# MASSIVE ACTION EQUALS MASSIVE RESULTS

*Learn the Critical Mental Framework to Focus Your Energy, Reach Your Goals Quicker and Live an Insanely Awesome Life*™

Sunil Saxena, M.D.

Copyright © 2017 Sunil Saxena, M.D. All rights reserved. No part of this publication may be reproduced, distributed, or transmitted in any form or by any means, including photocopying, recording, or other electronic or mechanical methods, without the prior written permission of the publisher, except in the case of brief quotations embodied in reviews and certain other non-commercial uses permitted by copyright law.

Project Summary

Massive Action Equals Massive Success: Learn the Critical Mental Framework to Focus Your Energy, Reach Your Goals Quicker and Live an Insanely Awesome Life

Authored by Sunil Saxena MD

Saxena Publishing, LLC

ISBN-13: 978-0692947081 (Custom Universal)
ISBN-10: 0692947086

# DOWNLOAD THE FREE AUDIO BOOK!

Just to say thanks for downloading our book, we'd like to give you the Audiobook 100% FREE!

Go to
www.saxenaspeaks.com/freeaudiobook

*Sunil Saxena, MD*

# BOOK DR. SAXENA
## TO SPEAK

Visit

www.saxenaspeaks.com

*Sunil Saxena, MD*

To my children,
Mia, Rohan, Gavin, and Dillon.
You guys are the reason I do everything I do.

I love you, peeps!

# Acknowledgments

To my editor, Elayne Wells Harmer: thank you for your excellent editing skills. Without you, this book could not have become a reality.

Thank you to all the authors—especially those mentioned in this book—who courageously dared to write their books and contribute knowledge to the world. Reading has made me who I am today!

# AUTHOR'S NOTE

In February 2015, I realized I had not accomplished what I was capable of during my years on this planet. I had just turned 45, which in my mind was the "halftime" of my life. From the time I was young, others have admired my potential, characterizing me as someone who "will do great things someday." Although I had accomplished a lot by others' standards, I couldn't say I had done "something great." By my standards, I had given a mediocre performance for 45 years. I earned an M.D., was a successful doctor, had four great children, and started six successful companies.

But I knew I was capable of more.

I have been given great talents, and as John F. Kennedy once said, "those to whom much is given, much is expected."[1] I take this charge seriously—I know I have more in the tank to make this planet a better place before I am gone.

As I looked back on my 45 years, I tried to understand what had worked well and what had not. This self-analysis and deep reflection resulted in a huge life change. I took what I call "massive action" and studied how I could improve. I hired a life coach and met with him every week for an entire year. Every day I carefully examined the good and the bad in my life. I read books and went to seminars. I

---

1 Address to the Massachusetts legislature, January 9, 1961 (*Congressional Record,* January 10, 1961, vol. 107, Appendix, p. A169).

thoroughly researched and studied every aspect of self-improvement and reaching your potential.

The result? I pinpointed which of my traits and behaviors had led to my successes and which ones were holding me back. I identified weaknesses and deficiencies. Since then, I have significantly improved in these areas by taking Massive Action[2].

What is Massive Action? Defining it and explaining its power to change is why I wrote this book. I want to share my experiences so that you, too, can gain valuable insights that will change your life. I can say without reservation that adopting a Massive Action mindset has been a critical aspect of my success.

You don't have to have the goal of becoming a billionaire or achieving worldwide fame to adopt the Massive Action mindset and lifestyle. No matter how big or modest your goals are, taking Massive Action will allow you to achieve your goals more quickly and easily, and with more certainty. This approach will make you a better person. It will give you the energy and momentum you need to not just live a life but *thrive* throughout your life.

In the following pages, I'll explain what Massive Action is, give you real-life suggestions on how to take it, and describe the hurdles to look out for along the way. I sincerely hope you find this book valuable and even life changing. These concepts changed my life—I'm confident they can change yours as well.

Sunil Saxena, M.D.
Washington, D.C.
August 2017

---

[2] When I'm talking about "massive action" the way I define it, I will refer to it as "Massive Action."

# CONTENTS

Author's Note ..................................................................................... vii

Section I: What Is Massive Action? ..................................................... 1
    Chapter 1: Taking Extraordinary Steps ........................................... 3
    Chapter 2: A 20X Mindset ............................................................... 5
    Chapter 3: A Little Extra ................................................................. 9
    Chapter 4: Go Big or Go Home ..................................................... 15
    Chapter 5: Swing Big, Miss Big ..................................................... 17
    Chapter 6: 168 Hours in a Week ................................................... 21
    Chapter 7: Three Weeks in Every Week ........................................ 25
    Chapter 8: The Un-Comfort Zone ................................................ 27
    Chapter 9: Grit .............................................................................. 33

Section II: How To Take Massive Action .......................................... 37
    Chapter 10: Identify Your Why ..................................................... 39
    Chapter 11: Keep the Right People Around You .......................... 45
    Chapter 12: Acquire Knowledge: Seminars, Books,
    and the Internet ............................................................................ 49
    Chapter 13: Establish Rock-Solid Inner-Core Beliefs .................... 53
    Chapter 14: Just Do It ................................................................... 57
    Chapter 15: Keep the Momentum ................................................ 59
    Chapter 16: Make It a Lifestyle ..................................................... 63
    Chapter 17: Make Rapid Decisions ............................................... 67
    Chapter 18: The 30-Day Challenge ............................................... 71
    Chapter 19: Develop Mini Habits ................................................. 75
    Chapter 20: Set a Schedule ............................................................ 79
    Chapter 21: Overwhelm Your Other Senses ................................. 83
    Chapter 22: Go Back to Basics ...................................................... 87

Chapter 23: Remove Fear ............................................................. 89
Chapter 24: Use Fear of Missing Out (FOMO) ...................... 93
Chapter 25: Don't Take Action for Action's Sake ..................... 95
Chapter 26: Set S.M.A.R.T. Goals ............................................ 97
Chapter 27: Review High-Level Goals Daily ......................... 103
Chapter 28: Eliminate and Outsource .................................... 105
Chapter 29: Block Uninterrupted Time ................................. 109
Chapter 30: Use a High-Level Strategy ................................... 111
Chapter 31: Live with Uncertainty ......................................... 115
Chapter 32: Modeling ............................................................ 119
Chapter 33: Stay in Peak State ................................................ 123
Chapter 34: Believe in Your Goals .......................................... 129
Chapter 35: "Persist Until" ..................................................... 133

**Section III: Hurdles To Taking Massive Action** ........................ 137
Chapter 36: The Invisible Force ............................................. 139
Chapter 37: You Are Enough ................................................. 143
Chapter 38: Negative Feedback .............................................. 147
Chapter 39: Bad Advice .......................................................... 151
Chapter 40: Bad Shit .............................................................. 155
Chapter 41: Little Action Equals Little Results ..................... 161
Chapter 42: Avoid Victim Mentality ...................................... 165

**Conclusion: Determine Your Destiny** ........................................ 169

# SECTION I:
# WHAT IS MASSIVE ACTION?

Sunil Saxena, M.D.

# CHAPTER 1:
# TAKING EXTRAORDINARY STEPS

*"The path to success is to take massive, determined action."*
—Tony Robbins[3]

Literally defined, "massive action" means taking big steps or doing big things. The term is a lot more complex than it initially seems, though. It's a nuanced point that takes time to truly understand, but it's well worth the extra effort.

Massive Action means doing everything it takes to get to your goal. It can mean giving 120 percent. It can mean going to great or extraordinary lengths to accomplish your dreams—or it can simply mean doing more than the next person.

The word *massive* is relative. Certainly, an elephant is massive compared to an ant, but is an elephant massive compared to the earth? It's clear that Massive Action must be compared to something for it to be deemed "massive."

In the following pages, I'm going to help you understand what this concept means at its deepest level, why it's so important, and

---

[3] Tony Robbins, Facebook page, January 31, 2015, https://www.facebook.com/TonyRobbins/posts/10153040938109060.

how to shift to a Massive Action mindset and lifestyle. I'll explain how taking this kind of action is different from and independent of accomplishing goals.

You cannot control the outcome of a certain event. You can, however, push as hard as possible on something you do have the ability to control: yourself. If your goal is to win the U.S. Open, you can't entirely control that specific outcome—but taking Massive Action will nevertheless give you stunning results and take your game to the highest level. Phil Mickelson, for example, has not yet won the U.S. Open, but he has taken Massive Action to improve his game and achieved incredible results—he's one of the greatest golfers of our time. When you focus your actions on things you can control, and do so over a long period of time, you will see extraordinary results. You will almost certainly accomplish your loftiest goals.

Massive Action is a mindset and a lifestyle. Without it, true success is not possible—but with it, anything is.

# CHAPTER 2:
# A 20X MINDSET

*"The only easy day was yesterday."*
—Motto of the U.S. Navy SEALs

Understanding and believing that you are capable of 20 times what you're currently accomplishing is a vital mindset if you want Massive Action to produce real results for you. The "20X" mindset must become a rock-solid inner-core belief (see Chapter 18). If your goals sound good to you, but you don't truly believe you have what it takes to achieve them, Massive Action will have limited results.

The 20X mindset comes from the Navy SEALs, elite warriors who are given the most difficult and dangerous missions, defending the United States of America. Their motto suggests that each day they must prove what they're capable of—they don't slack off or rest on past achievements. They have reached the highest level in the military by believing that their capabilities increase with each accomplishment. Whatever your focus, you must have this mindset if you want to succeed at the highest level.

The SEALs use mental, physical, and emotional challenges to prove to themselves that they are truly capable of 20X. Once you see that you are capable of 20X in one area, it becomes natural to believe you can do 20X in any area. That's how success begins. 20X is a foundational mindset that is critical for Massive Action to work.

As the Navy SEALs do, you can use physical and mental challenges that are not related to your primary field to prove to yourself that 20X is possible.

For example, if you can run one mile and I tell you that you're completely capable of running 20 miles, it may seem doubtful or even impossible to you. The story of the Fauja Singh, a man from India who *started* running marathons after the age of 100, comes to mind. He did not let anything, including age, stop him from starting a new journey. You just start doing it and push yourself farther every day. Before you know it, you're running 20 miles and you realize, *Wow, I am capable of doing 20 times what I thought I could.*

Similarly, if you make $100,000 a year and I tell you you're capable of making $2 million a year, it may seem far-fetched and unattainable. If you've conquered running 20 miles, though, it becomes easier for you to believe you can earn 20X what you are earning today. Confidence in one area carries over to others, and soon you realize you're extremely capable in many areas of your life. Have you ever noticed that successful individuals are often successful in multiple areas? Arnold Schwarzenegger was a seven-time Mr. Olympia, a Hollywood A-list celebrity, married to a Kennedy, governor of California, and an internationally recognized personality. He has often said that what he learned in bodybuilding carried over and made him successful in many other areas. He learned the concept of "sets and reps" as a bodybuilder, and applied it to everything in his life.

Similarly, things that are difficult for you, such as talking to strangers or public speaking, can be used as mental challenges to show that you are 20X more capable than what you think. Whatever you are the most afraid of is exactly what you should conquer first. This proves to *yourself* (don't do it to prove to anyone else) that you can achieve things you previously thought were unthinkable. It starts you down a path of success.

The late Arnold Palmer was initially terrified of flying. He overcame his fears and even became an expert pilot. He flew himself to many golf tournaments and other events, and would often take his friends along, including Jack Nicklaus.

Likewise, if you're deathly afraid of public speaking, you should take this on as a challenge—not with the goal of making public speaking your profession, but rather to prove to yourself that you can overcome this. Become the best speaker you can possibly be.

Interacting in social situations and talking to strangers used to be a big fear of mine. I struggled with it for more than 10 years, and I finally decided that I wanted to be able to talk to anybody, anywhere, any time. Having worked on this for years, I have reached that point. This newfound comfort has freed me up in social situations and allowed me to interact and network much better. More importantly, it proved to me that I can take on my most difficult challenges and succeed. I'm even developing a course called Social Dynamics on this exact topic.

Physical challenges such as running, push-ups, sit-ups, and chin-ups can also be used as the Navy SEALs do on a routine and regular basis. Personally, I could only do two push-ups before I started training. Now I can do 100 push-ups in two minutes or less—something I never thought possible but is routine and easy now. This confidence translates into everything else when I want to take on a difficult challenge. There's always that initial *"well, can I really do this?"* thought, but drawing on past successes of improving my social dynamics (talking to anyone, anywhere, anytime) and conditioning (push-ups), I immediately realize that I'm more than capable of taking on the next challenge that is 20X what I'm currently doing. The thought comes and goes in an instant and does not paralyze me from taking Massive Action.

Making 20X a rock-solid inner-core belief is a foundational element and must be present before you can see the results of taking Massive Action. You can put in a ton of effort, but if you don't truly believe you're capable of 20X, then you will instinctively find ways to sabotage yourself and not fully reap the benefits of putting in so much time and effort to accomplish your goals.

Here's an illustration. We all know people who do lots of things and appear very busy. You come back two or three years later, however, and they're essentially in the same situation—they haven't progressed.

A friend of mine dreamed of getting into the real estate investing game, reaping great financial rewards, and eventually giving up his primary job. I would see him and his wife at every real estate event in the area, and at every course I took, often paying for the highest level of training. What I noticed after a years, however, was that he really never got ahead. He and his wife did a lot of work and took Massive Action, but were stuck in the same place.

The problem was clear: he was missing that rock-solid inner core belief that he was in fact capable and worthy of achieving 20X his current situation. He outwardly projected that he and his wife could do it, but it was apparent that it was not something he really believed. This lack of self-belief and self-confidence prevented all the Massive Action from having its desired effect.

I've been through this process so many times and in so many different areas, it comes naturally to me at this point. Whenever I take on a new challenge that seems impossible—Jim Collins calls them BHAGs: Big Hairy Audacious Goals—I always experience some trepidation at first, but then I quickly draw upon my past experiences and get over it! Having accomplished and overcome many hurdles, I start taking Massive Action and don't let the initial fear cripple me. While the first 30, 60, or 90 days can be difficult, and it may even appear as if nothing is happening, I know that if I'm taking Massive Action, certain things will invariably materialize. I soon realize that I am actually doing what I thought was impossible just a month or a few months prior. I get through this phase quickly because I can draw upon my reference experiences.

Understand that to achieve mastery in anything typically takes 10 years. Malcolm Gladwell talks about the 10,000 hours rule. Ten years and 10,000 hours are only guidelines; everyone's experience will be different. Just remember to have a realistic timeframe. It's difficult in those first months, even years, to stick with things, because results can come slowly. Drawing from past experiences will help you understand this is how things work. You resist the temptation to declare defeat and move on to something else because you realize that sticking with things and even moving ahead with small victories is a start to Massive Results and fulfilling your dreams.

# CHAPTER 3:
# A LITTLE EXTRA

*"There's nothing wrong with ordinary. I just prefer to shoot for extraordinary."*

—Darren Hardy

The word *extraordinary* is a wonderful word to dissect and understand. The prefix *extra* comes from Latin, meaning "outside," so the literal translation is "outside of ordinary."

While the word *extraordinary* typically has a positive connotation, let's break it down further.

Most people spend their entire lives in pursuit of being ordinary. They want to be just like everybody else; they want to keep up with the Joneses. If the neighbors are doing it, then by all means it's a good idea. They want to fit in at work, at school, with their social circle. They want to be part of the "herd."

This instinct is genetically programmed into our outdated brain operating system. If you think about it, 10,000 years ago a human who did not fit in—who was outside of ordinary—risked a high chance of death. Back then you needed your group for survival. If you became "extraordinary," and the leader of the group didn't like your "extraordinaryism," you risked being ostracized from the group, which often meant death. No wonder genetic selection favored those humans who were more inclined to fit in. It is a powerful instinct programmed into us over thousands of years.

Like a lot of our instincts, however, they work against us in the modern world. We must learn to update our brain's operating system. Imagine using the first version of Windows operating system on your computer today—it just won't work. Your brain is running Windows 10,000 BC, and it's time for an update.

It can be difficult to reprogram some of these parts of your operating system. They are hardwired into you for survival. It is an uphill battle, but once you have done it, you are now playing with an OS that is modern and fresh and can easily beat those who have not taken the time or effort to upgrade.

If you look at Apple Computer, their entire "why" as a company is to challenge the status quo. They strive to be "outside ordinary." Steve Jobs in the 1980s was fired from his own company for challenging the system too much. After he left, the company dwindled down until it was almost out of business. They brought Steve back, and then Apple charted a course to become the most profitable company on the planet. Clearly, their core philosophy comes from Steve Jobs, who made a career of challenging the status quo and being extraordinary. Steve's death does concern me greatly for the future of Apple, but for now I'll enjoy writing this book on my brand-new Mac!

Apple does not have just customers—they have raving fans. I have seen many lines outside Apple stores worldwide when the company is releasing a new product. How many times have you seen this for a new Dell or Microsoft release?

Our public school is a perfect example of pushing everyone to be ordinary and often punishing those who dare to be extraordinary. The public school system in America is set up to make people ordinary by pushing them to the middle. The schools want under performers to move to the middle by increasing performance, and over-performers to move to the middle by hampering ambition, so that everything runs smoothly and harmoniously. In the most popular TED talk of all time, Ken Robinson explains this concept. He talks about how the public school system is killing creativity, which is another way of saying it's "killing" our extraordinary children—or rather, preventing them from being born in the first place.

In fact, the goal of organized society is to bring everybody into the middle to follow a set of rules. The problem with this thinking is that it discourages people from achieving great results. People are told their entire lives to stay on the normal path and follow the rules: go to school, get good grades, graduate from college, get an advanced degree if you really want to excel. Then get married, have 2.2 kids, and live happily ever after. In an organized society, daring to be different is often frowned upon.

Thankfully, those who accomplish great things don't pay attention to the conventions of organized society.

I don't know about you, but most people I come into contact with are bored out of their minds and are not happy at all. This is because they are not pursuing their passion, and they've become resigned to being ordinary. Since childhood, many of them have been taught to fear anything that is not normal.

We have to consciously understand this point and push ourselves to be outside ordinary. We have to upgrade our brain's operating system. Taking Massive Action in and of itself means being willing to be outside ordinary and suffer the negative consequences from the naysayers and haters who will certainly come. I'll explain this concept later, but if you don't have haters, then you're not doing it right. You need to go get some.

Stepping outside of your comfort zone to be extraordinary is where the magic happens. If you think you're going to be very comfortable while you achieve great success, think again. It doesn't work that way. In fact, accepting uncertainty and discomfort is a hallmark of a high achiever. High achievers are always challenging the system, receiving negative feedback, and being put in uncomfortable situations. If that's not your cup of tea, then Massive Action will not help.

Taking Massive Action squarely places you outside your comfort zone and makes you extraordinary. Since most people don't take Massive Action, this will cause your friends, family, coworkers, boss and acquaintances to question what you're doing.

This is exactly what happened to a man who worked at a video shop as a teenager. He was always telling everyone that one day he would make millions of dollars and drive a Porsche. Driving a Porsche was the symbol he used to keep his dreams alive and push forward. One day, the manager of the store pulled him aside and kindly gave him what he thought was good advice.

"Listen, son," the manager told him. "Don't get your hopes too high. All that does is lead to frustration and disappointment down the road. Trust me—I know."

The boy eventually left the small town, and seven years later, he came back as a young man—driving to the video store in his brand-new Porsche. The manager was *still* working there, and the two men had a very different discussion than the one they'd had years before.

Thankfully, the teenager had had the right mindset to ignore the manager's advice. After all, if you would not readily switch places with the person advising you, don't take the advice. Since the teenager clearly did not dream of being a video store manager, he did the right thing by politely thanking the manager for his advice, and then immediately dismissing everything he had said.

I hear this kind of well-meaning counsel all the time, even from my own family. Be careful, because your family can be your greatest enemy. They think they're telling you the right thing and doing what is in your best interest, but often they're giving you terrible advice.

It's important to understand that when you take Massive Action, become extraordinary, and start moving outside of your comfort zone, you'll find the road is not paved. You have to make your own path. It's not a smooth, paved road where you can drive 70 miles an hour in sheer comfort. It gets rough, and there are potholes, ditches, and other obstacles. Those who relish this and embrace it are the ones who are successful. Those who think this sounds dreadful are the ones who are better off being ordinary. The choice is yours.

I can still remember when my father, an architect, bought a few rental properties in the small town where we lived. He dreamed of making more money and having a nest egg for retirement. Within a year of purchasing the properties, he realized how much work it was to maintain them and all the headaches that came with that. His solution? He decided to get rid of the headaches, so he sold the properties at a loss. If he had kept the properties until the tenants paid off their mortgage, not only would he have made money every month but would have owned multiple properties by the time he was 60 years old.

My father's instinct was to get rid of the headaches and live a comfortable life. What resulted, however, was discomfort years later, when he did not have sufficient funds to enjoy life in retirement.

You must actually enjoy the headaches—*relish* them—and understand this is the path to achieving great success. Embrace the obstacles now, because they will allow you to achieve your dreams later. For many of you, this will be a 180-degree shift in your way of thinking.

Just the other day, a person in my improv class was commenting on how great it was to take this class, because he had met a diverse set of individuals who he never would have known otherwise. He had spent most of his adult life at the same job and with the same set of friends. He's a typical example of someone who's fine with simply moving comfortably through life and rarely striving to be extraordinary.

If you want to become extraordinary, you must operate outside your comfort zone, independent of what everyone else is doing. If everybody else is doing it, it's just not going to get you to the high-level success you desire. My friend took a small step outside his comfort zone by taking an improv class. Dive in with everything you've got!

I was talking to my teenage daughter the other day about typical high school activities, such as going to football games on Friday nights, going to prom, and having a normal and predictable daily schedule. She is doing none of the above—instead, she has set her sights on a higher goal and is laser-focused on achieving it. While some people—including her mother—think my daughter is missing out on the "high school experience," that's just their perspective. I could not disagree more.

It boils down to what she wants in life. If you want a "normal" life—where you fit in with the crowd—you'll never achieve any degree of high-level success. If you want to change the world or do something great, make sure you're being extraordinary. It's your choice—there's no right or wrong answer. It all depends on what kind of mark you want to leave on this earth.

Most people I know who achieved great things when they were

young did not fit into the norm. It's amazing how many ultra-successful people did not go to college: five of the world's 10 richest individuals do not have a college degree. While I am a strong believer in education, and I feel everybody should go to college and beyond, this is a perfect example of how doing something "outside of ordinary" will yield extraordinary results.

The motivational speaker Jim Rohn once said, "Formal education will make you a living; self-education will make you a fortune."[4] You must think beyond formal schooling and constantly self-educate. That's the only way to achieve a high level of success.

One of the fundamentals of taking Massive Action is continuously learning and educating yourself with small, incremental, continuous improvements. The Japanese call it *kaizen*.

Even if it's not directly related to what you're doing, you should always carve out a certain amount of time for continuing the educational process. I spend between $25,000 and $50,000 per year on self-education. This includes conferences, online seminars, training, personal coaching, and mentoring. How much do you spend?

---

4 Jim Rohn, Facebook page, July 20, 2015, https://www.facebook.com/OfficialJimRohn/posts/10155779714540635.

# CHAPTER 4:
# GO BIG OR GO HOME

*"Go big or go home. Because what do you have to lose?"*
—Eliza Dushku

Part of what makes up the Massive Action mindset and lifestyle is the "go big or go home" mentality. That means if you're going to do something, go all in: give it 100 percent of your enthusiasm and effort. Otherwise, what's the point of doing it? Why do something halfway? You do whatever it takes—and that usually means investing a large amount of action to move toward your goals. As we'll discuss later, what this does is build momentum, giving you the energy and motivation to persist and move forward.

If you're the kind of person who wants to be extremely cautious and take baby steps, that approach will likely not result in the proper Massive Action. Think of that methodology as applied to sports: when you take a full swing, it's so much easier to hit the ball. Whether you play golf, baseball, or volleyball, the concept is the same: if you come at it fully engaged, you'll hit the ball and hit it well.

As a tennis player, I have trouble when I play at half speed—it's much easier to hit the ball if I'm swinging at full speed, completely focused and engaged. Monica Seles and Maria Sharapova are examples of champion tennis players who put everything into every shot. Just listen to their grunts! Spectators at Wimbledon often complain that it interferes with their enjoyment of the match. That's when you know you're doing it right—when you get negative feedback because you're giving 100 percent! Put everything you have into every point in life and sit back and relish the complaints.

If you're not ready to do that, then go home, figuratively speaking. It's not worth undertaking a project or a goal if you're going to approach it cautiously and hedge your bets by taking a let's-wait-and-see attitude. Of course, there are always exceptions; certain areas in your life might call for a more cautious approach, but only you know which areas need that. Most of the time, however, you must dive in full force and not worry too much about the negative consequences. It just doesn't work otherwise—you're better off not doing it at all.

If you're taking Massive Action with a "go big or go home" mentality, you might undertake 10 things that move you toward your desired high-level success. If you have a wait-and-see approach, you might just try one thing at a time and never achieve success. Of the 10 things you try because of the right mental framework, number eight (for example) might really work and get you over the finish line of success. If you have a cautious attitude, however, you might give up after failing just a few times, never having gotten to number eight. Do everything in your power to achieve the results you want. You might be surprised to find that after just a few months of doing something, you'll realize what works and what doesn't. You'll be glad you tried something you otherwise would not have—and that something might be what gives you the success you desire.

# CHAPTER 5:
# SWING BIG, MISS BIG

*"I swing big with everything I've got. I hit big, or I miss big."*

—Babe Ruth

The swing-big, miss-big mentality is another essential part of taking Massive Action and a corollary of the "go big or go home" attitude. If you're going to do something, you might as well do it with everything you've got, even if your efforts result in an epic fail. Of course, there will always be critics who blast you when that happens. Take a look at those who criticize you, and examine their level of success. I guarantee that the vast majority of them are not successful. Those who *are* successful understand what you're doing and will support you.

When you don't take a shot, your chance of success is zero. Wayne Gretzky often observed that "you miss 100 percent of the shots you never take."[5] When you swing big, you will sometimes miss big. But

---

5 Charles Clay Doyle, *The Dictionary of Modern Proverbs* (New Haven, CT: Yale University Press, 2012).

sometimes you will connect, and the results will be massive. In fact, the results will be so big, they will eclipse all your misses combined.

Michael Jordan explains this beautifully.

"I've missed more than 9,000 shots in my career," he said in a 1997 Nike TV commercial. "I've lost almost 300 games. Twenty-six times I've been trusted to take the game-winning shot and missed. I've failed over and over and over again in my life. And that is why I succeed."

You must understand that when you're swinging big, you will often miss. In fact, you might even miss more often than you will hit. It's just that the hits are what people remember—and the hits are what will change your life. What we remember about Michael Jordan is his greatness and how he could make that game-winning shot again and again. We forget the 26 times he missed that shot at the last second. And even though he didn't always make the shot, overall he had the greatest career in the history of basketball.

Despite the occasional critic, your failures are not what most people see or remember. Unfortunately, *we* often remember them, and those memories can hold us back. There may be a few people who are quick to criticize or who focus on failure, but most people focus on success—almost to a fault. The human tendency to tell stories of success, especially "overnight" success, often makes us forget the hard work and failure that is part of the journey. Successful entrepreneurs know that success is what people value, but they also know that behind every success story are plenty of failure stories.

Jeff Bezos has built a company called Amazon (every heard of it?) by embracing this exact mentality. Amazon is constantly undertaking "big" initiatives to change the world. Bezos has built a culture where it is okay to fail. In most companies, employees get fired if they come up with some big scheme that fails. At Amazon, not only do such employees not get fired, they get a pat on the back and a hearty "good job!" This simple principle, in my opinion, is why Amazon is enjoying massive success. Jeff Bezos is not afraid to swing big and miss big—in fact he encourages it. And you know what? Every so often, Amazon connects on a big swing and changes the world.

Taking Massive Action allows you to develop the swing-big,

miss-big mindset. In fact, the two are almost the same thing. So just go for it—just do it!—and swing big even if you realize you may fail.

In baseball, getting a hit one-third of the time puts you in the Hall of Fame. What if I told you that you could achieve all your goals and enjoy all the success you desired—and you'd only be successful one-third of the time?

That is exactly how life works. You'll probably be unsuccessful two-thirds of the time and successful one-third of the time. Of course, the exact ratios will vary, but don't get hung up on the numbers. Focus on the fact that failure will occur. It's important to realize that when you're taking Massive Action, you will miss more than you hit.

Don't look at failure as a dead end or a reason to quit. Failure is an ingredient—a mandatory ingredient—to success. You cannot have success without failure. Every time you fail, you're a step closer to success. Recognize that every time you take action, you improve—even when you fail. When you understand the process and evaluate your failures, they will lead to and drive your success. This mindset allows you to celebrate your failures as much as you celebrate success.

We often take failure personally. We think that failure means we're not good enough to achieve our desired goals. We think that when we fail, we should quit. But the exact opposite is true. If we allow them to, failures will lead to success.

The cleaning solution Formula 409, for example, got its name because its inventor failed 408 times to get the formula right. On the 409$^{th}$ time, he got it right. Thomas Edison, one of the greatest inventors of all time, understood this mentality. At one point, a visitor to his lab said to him, "Isn't it a shame that with the tremendous amount of work you have done, you haven't been able to get any results?"

"Results?" he responded. "Why, man, I have gotten a lot of results! I know several thousand things that won't work."[6]

A quick look at Abraham Lincoln's life illustrates this point perfectly:

---

6 Frank Lewis Dyer and Thomas C. Martin, *Edison: His Life and Inventions* (New York: Harper & Brothers, 1910).

1816: The Lincoln family was forced out of their home; young Abe worked to help support the family.

1818: His mother died.

1831: Lost his job.

1832: Ran for state legislature—lost.

1833: Borrowed money to begin a business, and by the end of the year, the business was bankrupt. He worked for years to pay off the debt in full.

1834: Ran for state legislature again—won.

1835: His first love died, leaving him heartbroken.

1838: Sought to become speaker of the state legislature—defeated.

1843: Ran for his party's nomination for Congress—lost.

1846: Ran for Congress again—won. Went to Washington; did a good job.

1849: Sought the job of land officer in his home state—rejected.

1854: Ran for United States Senate—withdrew candidacy when process was deadlocked.

1856: Nominated for the vice-presidential position at his party's national convention—lost.

1858: Ran for U.S. Senate again—lost.

1860: Elected president of the United States.

That's an impressive list of failures—and they led to Abraham Lincoln becoming the president of the United States of America. Will you let failure stop you? Or will you recognize it is a natural part of success? The more often you swing—even if you miss—the faster you can work through your failures and create the environment you need for success.

## CHAPTER 6:
# 168 HOURS IN A WEEK

*"In any given day, we might not achieve the right balance. But in the whole of 168 hours, we can find space for anything that really matters."*[7]

—Laura Vanderkam

During my medical training, I quickly learned that there are 168 hours in every week. I became very familiar with that number, because there were many weeks during my training when I actually worked almost every one of them.

The philosophy of medical training in America is to have doctors in training live at the hospital (hence the word "resident"). The thinking is that if residents spend three years at the hospital, they will eventually learn enough to be competent doctors. The brutal schedule is also intended to weed out the "weak," those who cannot sustain the pressure of long hours required to take care of patients. This theoretically ensures the stick-to-it-ness that is required to hang in there and

---

[7] Laura Vanderkam, *168 Hours: You Have More Time Than You Think* (New York: Penguin Group, 2011).

do whatever it takes to make sure the patient gets the best outcome possible.

While the idea of using most of those 168 hours every week is part of the Massive Action mentality, today's method of medical training is missing a large component of this philosophy.

Just as in sports, practice makes you good. *Perfect* practice makes you great. You have to put in a LOT of hours towards your goal to get there—but in the proper way. Tony Robbins talks about taking massive, *determined* action. "Determined" is another way of saying it has to be done in the right way. That's what it takes to make sure the Massive Action is effective. Massive action has to be directed and focused towards the goal. A focused beam of light (a laser) can cut steel, but an unfocused light can at best light up a room.

My experience with medical training is that residents put in a lot of hours and essentially live at the hospital. That part of the Massive Action plan they have right. The problem, however, is that a majority of those hours, depending on the training program, are spent on useless tasks that don't really further your medical education or make you better at patient care. The long hours can be exhausting and actually hinder learning. When you have already worked more than a hundred hours and the week is not yet over, you can imagine a resident's level of fatigue. Fatigued individuals cannot perform well and certainly are in no state to learn.

Today's medical education is a perfect example of imperfect practice. While you will still improve and find your way through, the training is not producing the highest-quality doctors or high performers. Taking Massive Action is not just about putting in lots of time—massive results require targeted, efficient practice.

With 168 hours in a week, you can take 56 hours out for sleep (8 hours per day) and still have more than 100 hours per week to accomplish your goals. I bet you didn't think of it that way. The average person works a 40-hour work week. In the United States, we typically work closer to 50 hours because that's just our culture. Even at 50 hours, though, that's less than half the available hours to move towards your goal.

Taking Massive Action means doing whatever it takes to get to your desired high-level outcome. This also means understanding all the time available, and properly scheduling it so you optimize your time. Of course, too many hours on a consistent basis can lead to burnout and loss of motivation, but most people are not in danger of that happening. Most people are on the other side of the scale: they're only utilizing maybe 50 percent of available hours. They think they are working hard but are not even close to using the maximum time available.

It's amazing what you can get done when you understand what is available. Plan your days and your week so that you can use your time most effectively. Most people often have other commitments in terms of work and/or family. Determine what's important to you, because that will dictate how you are going to spend your available time.

I highly recommend writing your schedule down. Go through a typical week and start by slotting in your sleep time. Take an entire week and actually journal what you do every day by the hour. I bet you will be amazed at the difference between how you *actually* spend your time and how you *thought* you spent your time. After this week, you will have a good idea of how you are spending your time. Analyze your journal and organize your activities. Take a blank weekly calendar, slot in what you have to do, then find time for the new items you want to squeeze in. Make use of the remaining 112 hours, considering needed down time. Be realistic and put in what you think you can accomplish. Put in about 20 percent buffer time, because nothing ever works perfectly—plus humans cannot run at 100 percent efficiency for long. Once you do this, you will be amazed at how much time you actually have.

One thing I typically evaluate is drive time. When I have a drive that takes more than 30 minutes, I use that time productively. Drive time is a great opportunity to listen to audiobooks or make phone calls with your hands-free device. I get through an average of four books a month just using my drive time. This is just one example of maximizing your hours by carefully planning what you need to do. You can adjust on the fly as the day is evolving, but it's important to start with a high-level plan. If you don't plan out your day, you most likely will not accomplish much. If you start with a schedule, even if things go off course, you will still accomplish a lot.

Understanding that every week actually has 168 hours is the first step to using that time efficiently. With sleep time taken out, you still have over 100 hours per week. When you realize that, you see how much you can actually accomplish. If you keep doing this every week, imagine what you can accomplish in a month or year!

## CHAPTER 7:
# THREE WEEKS IN EVERY WEEK

*"Time is free, but it's priceless."*

—Harvey Mackay

In fact, every week actually contains three weeks! Most entrepreneurs understand this intuitively but may have never formally thought of it this way. People who don't take Massive Action have no clue what I'm talking about.

First, there's the regular workweek: Monday through Friday, approximately 8 a.m. to 5 p.m. Second, you have weekday evenings, approximately 6 p.m. to midnight. Third, you've got the weekend. Essentially, you can accomplish the same amount of work in any of these three periods.

People who don't have the Massive Action mindset cannot fathom working in the evenings or during the weekends. In the medical profession, working evenings and weekends is just assumed. Those who complain at the mere thought of working the "off" hours will not be the ones using Massive Action to accomplish massive goals.

Now, you don't always have to work evenings and weekends when you're taking Massive Action—unless you have a lot of commitments and you're trying to move into a different career or start a business. But once you start taking Massive Action and getting early results, you will likely want to work harder since you're seeing the path towards your ultimate goals. You'll want to be working evenings or weekends because you'll see the payoff. Working more can mean getting to your goals quicker.

Most average people do average things on weekends and evenings. Have dinner, watch TV, complain about their day, and that's about it. On weekends, they might go to a movie or a sporting event. Nothing organized, nothing focused, nothing moving them towards their goals.

One of my rules is that I can only stay up past 11 p.m. if I'm doing something productive. Just watching TV late at night is a waste of time and prevents my getting up early and accomplishing my tasks the next day. I can lose three to four hours that way—half a workday. If I am staying up late and wasting time, I have to work evenings and the weekend to make up for it. It's simply a choice you make when you are taking Massive Action.

It boils down to efficiency and learning what *you* can accomplish in a certain amount of time. Some people are more efficient and don't need as much time. Others need more time to accomplish the same tasks. There's nothing wrong with either way—you can take Massive Action no matter who you are or what time frame works for you. It's just a matter of understanding all the available resources and specifically realizing that there are three weeks available in every week. Plan and schedule accordingly so you're at your most productive level.

Use your three weeks in every week effectively, and you will have a triple advantage over others who do not understand this concept.

# CHAPTER 8:
# THE UN-COMFORT ZONE

*"Live where the magic happens—get out of your comfort zone."*

—Sunil Saxena, M.D.

It's critical that you get out of your comfort zone to achieve maximum results in life. Take a moment to truly understand and embrace this way of living, because it's critical that you have this mindset if you want Massive Action to work its magic. It must become a lifestyle, just as physical fitness should become a lifestyle if you really want it to work over the long term. It can't be something you do for a little bit then stop.

"Comfort zone" can be defined as a behavioral space where your activities and behaviors fit a routine and pattern that minimizes stress and risk. We all intuitively know the line between our comfort zone and "un-comfort zone," as I call it, but we're not always willing to admit those boundaries. We may think of ourselves as risk-takers—someone who pushes the limits. We may think we get out of our comfort zone easily and regularly. The truth is that few people embrace the deliberate practice of getting out of their comfort zone, and that's exactly why few people succeed at a high level in life.

Embracing the un-comfort zone can often be one of the most difficult things we do in life. As human beings, we are genetically hardwired to want to be comfortable. Ten thousand years ago when we lived in caves, if we got out of our comfort zone, we could die. Staying in our comfort zone was literally a life-and-death decision. It's clear why our ancestors who survived embraced comfort and security. This is why it is so difficult to get up on a cold, dark winter morning. Our Neanderthal ancestors worked hard to stay in a warm, safe environment.

In today's world, it is much more important to get up, get going, embrace the cold, and take Massive Action. Your body will fight you at every turn, telling you to stay in bed (or keep the same job, or live in the same town your whole life, etc.), since that is where comfort and security live. Your body does not know any better and is just trying to survive. Your outdated brain OS (Windows 10,000 BC) will do everything it can to make you stay in bed because it is hard wired with a survival-first mentality. It does not care that you want a six-pack and that requires getting up and going to the gym. It just wants to survive.

Personally, I can get out of bed much more easily on a warm, sunny summer day than I can on a cold, dark winter day. Getting up at 6 a.m. in the summer is relatively easy for me, but dragging myself out of bed at 6 a.m. in the winter feels like the biggest fight of my life. However, once I'm up and about, it's hard to remember why it was such a big deal. Despite being as "smart" as I think I am, this scene plays out daily in the wintertime, and this pattern repeats itself every year.

The first step to taking Massive Action and getting out of this cycle is to understand 1) that it exists, and 2) *why* it exists. Once you understand the underlying reasons for the difficulty of change and discomfort, you can take action to give your body what it wants—while you get what *you* want. In my example of waking up in the winter, I can do a few things to help make it easier: I program the heat to come on two hours before my alarm goes off, I set bright lights to automatically turn on, and I have a cup of freshly brewed coffee waiting for me in the kitchen—so I have to get out of bed. These are all things that provide the comfort your body wants while your brain gets the satisfaction of getting up early to get work done.

In modern times, getting out of your comfort zone is a good thing. It doesn't have the dire consequences that it did 10,000 years ago. Training your mind to want to regularly visit your un-comfort zone today is something you must do if you want to be successful at a high level.

We all have different areas that stretch us out of our comfort zone. It's not the same for everyone. Most people do find it much more difficult to get up in the winter versus the summer, but some truly feel no difference. It is important to "know thyself," as Peter Drucker talks about so well in his book *Managing Oneself*, and to understand what causes us to feel stress and risk.[8] Certain triggers let us know when we are out of our comfort zone. A large portion of the world's population would almost rather die than speak publicly. It is important to understand, however, that this type of stress is a good thing, and we must learn to embrace and overcome it.

Other types of stress, such as chronic anxiety from financial hardship, are detrimental to our emotional and mental well-being, and will prevent us from reaching our goals. In those situations, we should work to solve the underlying problem. In other words, pushing yourself to become a master public speaker (if this makes you uncomfortable) will do wonders for your life in so many unrelated areas, but living in a state of chronic stress (such as financial hardship) just because you want to challenge and overcome obstacles will weaken your ability to perform in many areas of your life. I am talking about specific things such as public speaking that can be overcome in a set timeframe, not chronic stressors.

One of the huge advantages of taking Massive Action is that it often overwhelms your brain and allows you to get out of your comfort zone more easily. Additionally, it often produces results quickly, which then gives you the confidence to keep pushing harder and harder and move further and further out of your comfort zone. It essentially builds momentum, which is the rocket fuel that can propel you into the un-comfort zone—where success happens.

---

8  Peter F. Drucker, *Managing Oneself* (Cambridge, MA: Harvard University Press, 2008).

Talking in social situations such as a party is another great example of good stress. Many people find this terrifying. Think back to the last time you were in a social situation and felt some degree of stress and risk. The longer you waited to open your mouth and start talking to someone, the more that feeling of stress and risk built up within you. You started thinking about how people would react and started to envision all the negative reactions.

The reality is that you built up the situation in your mind *way* beyond the reality of the situation. It's amazing how quickly this can happen. You can start by feeling relatively comfortable, and within just a few seconds, you can become terrified simply because of the thoughts in your head. Just ask any guy who has wanted to talk to a girl he finds attractive. Things can go from calm and comfortable to terrifying in a matter of seconds.

This is where taking Massive Action can be the solution to the problem. When you know you are entering a stressful social situation, force yourself to start talking immediately (I call it the three-second rule—more on that later), and keep talking to anyone who will listen. Sometimes that means talking to the front desk person, the valet, or someone who is working the event. Just start talking. This will overwhelm your thinking mind and stop the unfounded fear from taking root.

Getting outside your comfort zone is where the magic happens. It's something you must actively seek out and make part of your lifestyle. If talking to people in public or learning to dance terrifies you, that's exactly what you must do. Successful people run toward the burning building (un-comfort zone), while the average person runs away from it as fast as possible because of an instinctual self preservation reflex.

Taking Massive Action and getting out of your comfort zone and overcoming fears will lead to success. It will allow your actions to produce the results you desire.

Every time you overcome a fear and get out of your comfort zone, it teaches you (specifically your unconscious mind) what you are capable of doing. It teaches you there is nothing to be fearful about. It becomes easier every time you do it. You can pull from your past experiences when you are having difficulty, and it will help you overcome whatever you face in the future. It is amazing how powerful this simple concept can be. But even so, people have tremendous difficulty getting out of their comfort zone. We are genetically programmed to resist this—it often feels like we're jumping off a building to certain death.

This is just fear, and it's important to push through this. Every time you push through fear successfully, it becomes easier and easier. You get to a point where getting out of your comfort zone and taking action is no longer a big deal. It's a great place to live your life. You just need to train your unconscious mind to trust your conscious mind. There will be a struggle between your unconscious mind, which resists the un-comfort zone, and your conscious mind. Every time you go through this cycle, your unconscious mind becomes more "comfortable" with the concept of being "uncomfortable," and it won't fight nearly as hard. Your unconscious mind now becomes your partner in success.

# CHAPTER 9:
# GRIT

> *"Grit is sticking with your future—day in, day out, and not just for the week, not just for the month, but for years."*
>
> —Angela Lee Duckworth

A nother essential element of Massive Action is grit: applying a high level of effort over a period of time. Another way to say this is "perseverance and passion for long-term goals."[9] Merriam-Webster defines it as "firmness of mind or spirit: unyielding courage in the face of hardship or danger."

Author Angela Duckworth notes that anyone wanting to take Massive Action and achieve Massive Results must sustain their effort over a long period of time. Any successful company or individual illustrates this principle—the timeline to their success almost always involves great effort for a long time. Even "overnight success" stories,

---

9 Angela Lee Duckworth, et. al. "Grit: Perseverance and Passion for Long-term Goals." *Journal of Personality and Social Psychology*, no. 92 (6) (2007): 1087–1101. doi:10.1037/0022-3514.92.6.1087

when examined closely, include years of action, failures, and refusal to give up.

A wonderful example is Jelena Ostapenko, the first tennis player from Latvia to win a Grand Slam tournament and the first unseeded player to win the French Open since 1933. (Translation for non-tennis players: that's a big deal.)

In tennis, as in all sports, up-and-coming stars break through every so often as the new generation claims their rightful spot. Jelena started playing tennis at age five and won the French Open at age 20. In other words, it took her 15 years to become an "overnight" success. Her youthful demeanor makes it seem like this "kid" who just started playing tennis won the French Open, but that's not the case at all. In fact, she is a 15-year-veteran of the sport.

Her victory brought tears to my eyes, because I understood the massive efforts that had gone into her success. This was a childhood dream coming true, something she had worked incredibly hard to achieve for the last 15 years. I don't know her personally, but I can guarantee she had many up and downs, along with many moments of doubt. However, she kept her eyes on the prize and kept moving forward. She displayed indomitable spirit and grit.

If you're not getting at least small wins over time, it's difficult to maintain effort over such a long period of time. Thankfully, taking Massive Action almost always results in some degree of success, and those small wins provide fuel to continue. High-level success is a long and difficult road, but every small achievement sustains you along the way. Understanding the concept of grit and the importance of maintaining it over time is one of the most important variables in success. Understanding this one concept can separate the successful from the unsuccessful.

People often point to talent as an essential part of success, and while talent never hurts, I believe it's only about 10 percent of the equation. Applying yourself and staying true to your mission over time is much more important. Pete Rose, one of the greatest baseball players of all time, mentioned this when he talked about how many players had more talent than he did, but they hadn't won the championships and awards he had won. He observed that simply staying in the game far outweighs talent.

History books are littered with people who had enormous talent but never amounted to anything. I know people like that, and I am sure you know a few people who fit the mold as well. In fact, when you look at highly successful people, you often discover that their talent is not even that great.

When given a choice, I will always bet on a person with a high degree of grit over someone with a high degree of talent. U.S. President Calvin Coolidge has often been quoted as saying the following:

Nothing in the world can take the place of persistence. Talent will not; nothing is more common than unsuccessful men with talent. Genius will not; unrewarded genius is almost a proverb. Education will not; the world is full of educated derelicts. Persistence and determination alone are omnipotent.

My daughter is an aspiring singer-songwriter, so I have become familiar with the music industry. You'll find countless examples of people in the music business who don't have the best voices yet have achieved a high level of success. Bob Dylan, Bruce Springsteen, and Tom Petty are perfect examples of individuals who may not be the best singers but have grit in abundance.

Having grit—or applying a high level of effort over a sustained period of time—is a foundational element of taking Massive Action. Grit allows you to keep going, and when you keep going, you'll achieve success—even if it's well down the road, years after beginning your journey.

# SECTION II:
# HOW TO TAKE MASSIVE ACTION

# CHAPTER 10:
# IDENTIFY YOUR *WHY*

*"People don't buy what you do, they buy why you do it."*
—Simon Sinek

Before you can take Massive Action, it's vital to understand why you're doing it. Making such a big change can be difficult for many reasons, including the time commitment involved and the pressures that naturally exist when creating change. When you understand your *why*, you become motivated and committed to taking the action you've identified.

Each of us has our own reasons for doing something, and we need to take the time to understand those reasons. Identify a methodology to help you pinpoint what is truly important to you and why you're doing what you do. Clarity and focus are essential for taking Massive Action. If you're not clear on what you want to achieve, taking Massive Action is like the shotgun approach: a lot of effort shot randomly in different directions.

I lacked clarity and focus when I first started making life changes. For several years, I was simply drifting, not really knowing what I wanted to accomplish in the next phase of my life. I'd accomplished a lot and was happy with where I was, but I knew there was more I could do and give. I hired a life coach and spent an entire year trying to gain clarity and focus on what I wanted to do next with my life. It was an incredible experience.

After a year of working with my coach on a weekly basis, I had the precise focus I needed to take Massive Action. I set out to do everything I could to reach the goals I'd set for the next chapter of my life. I started reading books and investigating multiple opportunities. I started to take Massive Action with the goal of figuring out what my end goals would be. I'm happy to report that incredible things have happened since that time, and I'm well on the way to achieving my current overall long-term goals.

Identify the end results you want, and you'll gain certainty about the right path for you. Taking Massive Action requires consistent effort, time, and grit. Without a solid *why*, you will likely quit before you achieve the desired results of making such an enormous change.

*Start with Why*[10] is a must-read for anybody who is serious about taking Massive Action. In this book, author Simon Sinek explains that understanding and connecting with your *why* is actually biology at work. You want to connect with your deep "reptilian brain," or limbic system—the old brain that evolved well before our rational-thinking neocortex.[11] This is the part of our brain that acts quickly and is driven by emotion, that instinctively tells us to run or fight if we are being attacked. It's the part of our brain that is wired to keep us alive. It has evolved to favor speed over intelligence when survival is at stake.

If you've ever made a decision based purely on instinct or emotion, this was the part of your brain that was acting. Rational decisions are made by the neocortex; emotional decisions are made by the reptilian brain. Sometimes our rational decisions are in sync with our emotions, and sometimes they are not. When you connect your *why* with your emotions, your ability to take Massive Action increases dramatically. Your instincts and emotions will be working with you,

---

10 Simon Sinek, *Start With Why: How Great Leaders Inspire Everyone to Take Action* (New York: Penguin Group, 2009).
11 A part of the cerebral cortex concerned with sight and hearing in mammals, regarded as the most recently evolved part of the cortex.

not against you. When your emotions support what you are doing, taking Massive Action becomes easier.

If you've ever started something you knew was good for you but your efforts fizzled out (like losing weight or beginning an exercise program), your reptilian brain most likely did not process your big *why*. Eventually your primitive programming won out, and your reptilian brain decided the effort wasn't worth it.

Connecting your *why* to this deep emotional center in your brain is the key to success.

When I decided to get in shape a few years ago, my fear of dying connected with my deep emotional center and became my big *why*. Before that, I had often started a fitness program, working out for weeks or even months at a time, but eventually giving up. I did not have a strong *why*. But in 2016, my blood pressure spiked to life-threatening levels, and I finally realized I had to get control of my diet and begin a regular exercise program. I immediately began a 30-day challenge, and since that moment, I have consistently worked out and eaten healthy. The real fear of death connected with my emotional brain and pushed me to make these behaviors a consistent part of my life. Before this, nothing had worked.

Understanding how your actions and behavior influence those around you should also be part of your *why*. When you're successful at taking Massive Action, your family, friends, children, and others around you benefit as well. Success—however you define it or wherever you achieve it—makes a difference to those close to you.

A friend of mine was a jock in high school who struggled just to get Cs. In his 20s, however, he joined the Keller Williams sales organization, and today he is the top-selling agent in his Kentucky hometown. Although academics weren't his thing, he had the typical gritty get-the-job-done mentality often found in football guys. That mentality—combined with him identifying his *why*—provided the combination that led to his superstar success.

He talks a lot about why he does what he does. The number-one reason he sells real estate is to provide his family with the lifestyle he never had. He throws an annual Kentucky Derby party that costs about $50,000. That's a lot of money, but he looks forward to this party every year. He enjoys every minute, and he loves providing his family, close friends, and business associates with a unique experience they could not have had otherwise. His hard work and success allows him to do these types of things.

My friend understands that an important part of his *why* is to support those around him. No matter who you are or what you are trying to accomplish, part of your *why* should include identifying ways that your success can support and help those in your life who you care about.

In fact, the Keller Williams organization is a great example of that principle. The organization talks about building a "business worth owning" for a "life worth living." Sure, selling houses can be fun, but like all jobs, it's only a means to an end. Whatever we do to earn a paycheck, the real reason we are working is to create a life worth living.

Understand your big *why*. Take Massive Action. Support those around you. This is a formula for a life well lived.

Even before I had a family, I knew my *why* for success and financial freedom was to support my children. In addition to providing for them when they were young, I knew they would someday develop their own passions, and I wanted to fully support them in those endeavors. I knew this even before they were born.

Fast-forward 15 years later: my son is a competitive golfer, and my daughter is a singer/songwriter. Both of them have aspirations to perform professionally. My main reason for what I do is to support them to make *their* dreams come true. All the hard work I have invested in the past allows me to have the money—and, more importantly, the time—to support them 100 percent now.

Having that time and financial freedom is huge. And I've identified a new *why*: location freedom. My daughter will likely go on tour at some point in her career, and my son may attend college far away. I want to support them every step of the way, and that means having a business that isn't tied to one geographical location.

When the going gets tough as I work to create that business, I remember why I do what I do, and push though the difficulties. Of course, I recognize that my kids may or may not be successful at the highest level, but I can look back no matter the outcome and know I did all I could to support them. That is what's important to me. If financial or location pressures prevented me from supporting them 100 percent, I might always wonder, "What if?" What if I had worked harder and provided more support? Would that have made a difference in their success? Because I've taken Massive Action to get where I am, I don't have to wonder.

Success begets success. We see it happening all around us: the rich get richer, and the poor get poorer. Once you are on the upward spiral of success, you keep accomplishing more—and it helps those around you achieve success as well.

An important, often-overlooked aspect of success is your mindset. When you start achieving success, you know you have the right mindset. That positive attitude and outlook rubs off on those around you, especially your family.

A great example of this mindset is reading two to four books a month. My goal is to read at least two books a month, but I typically read four books. At a very young age, my children adopted this same simple habit. I can only imagine how different my life would be today if I had started reading this many books when I was younger. I am often asked for the one piece of advice I would give someone who wants to be successful. My advice is simple: read a minimum of one book every month. When you read, you gain information and education, develop discipline, and create the mental framework needed for success. Of course, you need to do more than read books, but in my opinion, reading is the most important thing you can do to get started on the right path. Reading is just one example, but at the heart of success is a mental framework of how to learn and apply knowledge in pursuit of a certain goal.

Of course, success doesn't just allow you to help and support those around you—it first affects *you*. Initial success creates a foundation on which you can continue to build great things. Look around. You'll see numerous examples of people who became successful in one area and then used that success to achieve in other areas.

For example, over the course of a decade, Arnold Schwarzenegger was named Mr. Olympia seven different times. He then parlayed that success into building an A-list Hollywood career. He continued his record of success in politics by becoming the governor of California.

I am living proof of this same principle. The success I achieved as a doctor led to my success in business, which now provides me with other entrepreneurial opportunities, including writing this book and sharing my story. Without my initial success, I never would have been able to do this.

No matter what your big *why* is, remember that an important part of that needs to include supporting those you care about, as well as supporting your future success.

# CHAPTER 11:
# KEEP THE RIGHT PEOPLE AROUND YOU

*"You are the average of the five people you spend the most time with."*

—Jim Rohn[12]

When you're taking Massive Action, it's critical to make sure you have the right people around you if you want success. Think of them as multipliers of your Massive Action. If you have the right people, they will multiply your action in a positive way. If you have the wrong people, they will detract from your action in a negative way.

Take inventory of the five people you spend the most time with, because they are the ones who have the greatest influence on you. Are they friends? Family? Is your spouse one of them? Maybe people at work? Are they taking Massive Action? If the answer is yes, then you have some great people around you, and it should be much easier for you to adapt the Massive Action lifestyle.

---

12  Jim Rohn, Facebook page, September 6, 2014, https://www.facebook.com/OfficialJimRohn/posts/10154545230540635.

If the answer is no, then they are not the right people. You must figure out a way to find the right people and spend more time with them. This can be done through networking groups, associations, online forums, mentoring, coaching, and even online Facebook groups. It's amazing the amount of technology and reach we have these days and unique ways to spend time with the right people.

It can seem harsh at times, but the wrong people will sabotage the effects of your Massive Action. Even if they are longtime friends or family members, it is critical that you separate your time from them if they are not the right people. You don't have to cut them out 100 percent, but you must limit your interactions. It will absolutely have an effect on your Massive Action.

One area I see this phenomenon play out is in long-term relationships such as marriages. One person might be the type to take Massive Action or becomes that person after marriage, while the other person is not. This creates friction and tension. I've seen marriages (including mine) fall apart for this very reason. When you take Massive Action, you are a different person from the average Joe. This can cause trouble in your closest relationships. If you want success, you have to be willing to understand this concept and identify ways to deal with it.

This is also common in sports. My son is a competitive golfer and is always looking to improve. He is taking Massive Action with the goal of becoming a professional golfer. He plays at a local club that has many kids in the same situation—junior golfers who are literally some of the best in the world, with the same goals and mindset of taking Massive Action. He is lucky to have found such a great environment. He can naturally spend a lot of time with the right people.

Specifically take time to identify the five people you spend the most time with. Just like in a fantasy football league, analyze each player and see if they're the right fit for the team *you're* trying to create. If so, the player stays; if not, figure out a way to replace that player with somebody who is taking Massive Action and moving towards high-level goals like the ones you want.

Write this down and rate each person from 1 to 10. The goal is to get to all 10s. You may start far from this, but this is okay. Start on the road to gathering an all-star team around you. After all, who doesn't want to be surrounded by 10s?

I recently did this while going through an exercise to find my real *why*, and I was able to identify the characteristics of the individuals I wanted around me. I realized I did not have the right people around me, so I set out to find them. I identified the following characteristics in individuals I want around me:

- Unwilling to settle for the status quo
- Driven by goals
- Diverse and inclusive of people and ideas
- Think at an intellectual level that challenges me
- Handle my desire to never stop growing and learning
- Have the tools/gifts to be better, but may need some guidance maximizing them

People often hear this and think, "Yeah, yeah, yeah, I've heard that, and I'll work on it." I can't express enough how important it is to actually *write this down* and make sure that you've got the right people in place.

Podcasts and books are great ways to gather the right people around you without actually being physically with them. I listen to a phenomenal business podcast on a regular basis. I get to "spend time" with the right people when I want to—and it doesn't cost me a penny. I'm continually amazed at how I learn critical nuggets in almost every episode I listen to. I would be happy if I got such a nugget weekly or even monthly—one little piece of knowledge or insight can change your life.

Books are another great way to spend time with the right people. I typically read four books in an average month, with a goal of two books per month at minimum. I often reread the best books. You get to spend time with the right people for hours—again, on your terms and at a minimal cost. If, like me, you who have trouble reading physical books, check out audiobooks. This format has changed my life since I can get through a book on a plane flight or a longer drive out of town. I can consume an audiobook for hours, but when I read physical books I have about a 30-minute attention span. My daughter is the exact opposite and much prefers physical books. Just figure out what works best for you and get started.

If you're trying to improve in life and are serious about taking Massive Action in different areas, it's critical to have support from at least one person in each area. That person can support you in that specific area and help you achieve the right mindset.

Think about this and take it seriously. It is a critical factor that will lead to success if done properly.

# CHAPTER 12:
# ACQUIRE KNOWLEDGE: SEMINARS, BOOKS, AND THE INTERNET

*"Education is the most powerful weapon you can use to change the world."*

—Nelson Mandela[13]

It's normal to have different aspects of your life in different stages. For example, your career may be successful, but your journey to physical fitness is just beginning. Or you feel comfortable and confident speaking publicly, but the thought of talking one-on-one with a stranger terrifies you.

When you're starting your journey in any pursuit, your most important tool is knowledge. We live in an incredible age where massive amounts of information—much of it specialized information—is available at our fingertips, essentially for free. You have heard of the Internet, right? When you are in the knowledge-acquisition phase of your journey, be open to all sources of knowledge and devour as much as you can. Since you are early in your journey, you don't know what source or type of knowledge will be the key to your success, so take

---

13 Nelson Mandela, *Notes to the Future: Words of Wisdom* (New York: Atria Books, 2012).

in as much as possible. With time, the path you should follow will become clear.

Obtaining knowledge is one thing; implementing it is another. That's where many people get bogged down. Those of us who love to learn are good students, but often we're not very good implementers.

You can acquire knowledge through a variety of sources. I personally recommend taking as many classes and seminars as you can, online or in person. Both provide the knowledge that you need. I have found, however, that my best contacts come from in-person seminars. And the best knowledge doesn't always come from the actual seminar—I often find the golden nuggets come from the people you talk with *during* the seminar.

For example, I recently attended a conference on social media. I overhead two individuals talking about how to capture great video they could use on a social media platform. Drones are relatively new, and they both had recently begun learning about and experimenting with drones. They compared notes and shared what was working for them.

While this may seem insignificant, the fact that they were able to interact with someone who shared a common passionate pursuit helped them both. A single nugget might have changed the way they captured film, changing their online content from a dismal failure to super successful. You never know what piece of information or person you meet will make the difference. Having an open mind and continuing to learn everything you can is key.

Now, most of what I have learned during the knowledge-acquisition phase hasn't helped me in the long run. However, to find those gold nuggets, I have to be searching for knowledge of all kinds. If you try to discriminate from the get-go, you'll miss important pieces of gold that can lead to success.

Books are another incredible source of knowledge. To begin with, I highly recommend reading at least one book every month on the specific area you're trying to master. Additionally, read other genres: classics, self-help, general knowledge, even fiction. The point is to simply read. I often find that even when I'm reading non-business-related books, I learn concepts that apply beautifully to the area that I'm working on. What I read provides a different perspective, and that slight alteration in the way I see something can lead to massive success in that given field.

The Internet is literally a game changer from a knowledge-acquisition standpoint. I grew up in the 1980s and 1990s when acquiring knowledge looked very different. I remember going to the library in middle school to do research for a book report, and started by opening up the *Encyclopedia Britannica*. Typically the information was many years out of date, but we went with whatever was printed in the encyclopedia. We did our best not to plagiarize, but basically we were summarizing what we found in one resource.

In the 1990s, I remember trying to find information about different companies when I was investing in stocks. The best information came from Charles Schwab; the organization would fax a four-page summary of certain companies upon request. Obtaining information was time-consuming and complicated—and outdated as soon as I received it. The information also came from a single source and could be biased.

This is what makes the Internet a game-changer when you're taking Massive Action. Once you determine what topic you'd like to study, you can begin acquiring knowledge within seconds. Within minutes, you can gather more information than you can consume in days. And that's not all—you can also find experts who can help you with your exact situation, and classes and seminars you can attend to learn more.

Recently I was learning about Instagram ads and how to use them to build an audience for musicians. This approach is relatively new, and I had no experience. Within a few hours, I read blogs, watched YouTube videos, and gained a fairly solid understanding of Instagram ads. It was all free, and I never left my computer. On-demand knowledge—what a great thing!

With the Internet, you don't have to travel to conferences or spend lots of money to find experts who know what they are doing. We live in an age where information is available at our fingertips. In fact, you don't even have to be at your computer—you can pull up this information on your phone.

If you're not taking advantage of this plethora of free information at your fingertips, you're missing out on an enormous resource. Somebody is trying to hand you the keys of the kingdom, and you're basically saying, "No, thanks. I'll stay here in a job that I hate and a life that is going nowhere." That's crazy! Seek and acquire this knowledge, and improve your life.

The Internet also offers great resources for a price. Quality online classes and trainings are invaluable. Again, in the old-school way of learning, you traveled to conferences and consumed content on a predetermined schedule. Today you can find incredible training programs online that include videotaped conferences and lectures. You can watch these at 3 in the morning or 10 at night—whenever your schedule allows. The Internet allows you to acquire knowledge during times that fit your availability rather than the availability of the content provider.

The information you find on the Internet is staggering. For instance, the battery in my key fob was dead. Cars these days are quite complicated, and it's difficult to figure out what's going wrong. I went to YouTube, and within minutes found a video of someone walking me through the exact process of starting my car—the exact make and model—without a battery in the key fob. Before, I would have had to call AAA or the dealer, and likely would have been stranded for hours while trying to solve the problem. Thanks to the amazing amount of knowledge available on the Internet, I was able to take action, figure out the solution, and be on my way within minutes.

Knowledge acquisition allows you to take Massive Action. Begin by developing the knowledge base necessary to make decisions and move toward your goal. Without knowledge, you are unable to implement action in any meaningful way. The resources you need are at your fingertips!

# CHAPTER 13:
# ESTABLISH ROCK-SOLID INNER-CORE BELIEFS

*"Your belief will help create the fact."*

—William James[14]

Belief is divided into three levels. If you want Massive Action to work its magic, you must have Level Three belief, which I call rock-solid inner-core belief (RSICB).

Level One is disbelief. This level is easy to understand—if you don't believe you're going to become the president of the United States, you probably won't be. If you truly believe something isn't going to happen, chances are high that it's not going to happen.

Level Two is more difficult to understand and to evaluate. I call this level "false belief": when you outwardly pretend to believe something, but deep down inside, you don't believe. Individuals at this level can fool others—and even themselves. Outwardly they project a lot of

---

14 William James, *The Will to Believe* (CreateSpace Independent Publishing Platform, 2016).

confidence and make others believe they truly have RSICB. I've often found myself at this level.

With false belief, people may say, "Oh, sure, I can do this." But you can see in their eyes that they're not really sure it's going to happen. At this level, individuals often hesitate and qualify. Instead of saying, "Of course it's going to happen," they think about it a little bit.

Or they might say, "Well, I guess I can do this as long as . . ." and then they list a few reasons they may fail. They are qualifying themselves, or hedging their bets, and that indicates doubting. If you truly believe something, there is no need to qualify. At the false-belief level, you can often fool others, and even yourself. You cannot, however, fool your subconscious mind. If you have false belief, your subconscious mind knows that you don't believe, even if you have convinced your conscious mind otherwise.

It takes effort to move up to Level Three: firm, rock-solid inner-core belief, the only level where Massive Action can produce results. RSICB is the true conviction we are looking for. It means you talk about something without a moment of hesitation. Here's a simple example:

A friend or co-worker asks, "Hey, can you grab me a coffee from Starbucks? I really need it to keep going this afternoon."

You say, without hesitation, "Of course, no problem. I'll be right back."

That's RSICB. You have no doubt you can get the coffee and bring it back.

But you might not feel as confident if someone asks, "Hey, do you think you can get this project done by the end of the day?" You may hesitate and start qualifying, saying, "Well . . . I'm not sure it will happen unless X, Y, or Z happens too."

For Massive Action to result in the massive results you want, you need rock-solid inner-core belief. That kind of belief is what makes the big stuff happen.

If RSICB were in the dictionary, Muhammad Ali's picture would be right next to the definition. He truly believed in everything he did in his life, not just boxing. He exuded fearless confidence and inner-core belief. "I am the greatest," he said. "I said that even before

I knew I was. I figured that if I said it enough, I would convince the world that I really *was* the greatest." The important thing is that *he* believed he was the greatest—it was just a matter of proving this to the world.

Muhammad Ali's deep belief unquestionably contributed to his massive success in boxing and beyond.

If you struggle with developing RSICB, you can do something about it: every day, reaffirm that you really can do whatever it is you want to do. I call it "believe it until you *know* it." Keep pushing yourself until you know deep down in your heart that you can do it, until you can say it without a moment of hesitation. Remember, your subconscious (or reptilian brain) must believe as well. Once you believe on every level, amazing things start to happen.

## CHAPTER 14:
# JUST DO IT

*"Just do it—even if you suck at it."*
—Twist on a Nike ad campaign

An essential part of taking Massive Action is developing a just-do-it mentality. The slogan made famous by Nike is, in my opinion, the best three-word slogan ever. When you have a just-do-it mentality, you take Massive Action. This slogan is not just for athletes—anyone can achieve tremendous success and impressive results with this mentality.

While thinking things through is an important part of achieving success, most people take thinking to an extreme. When I'm uncomfortable and out of my comfort zone, I often find myself overthinking an action and finding reasons not to do it. Maybe I'll decide not to attend an event because I "need to get up early" so I can have a productive day—even though I'm typically in bed by 10 or 11 p.m. even when I do attend events. I *over*think it and look for excuses and reasons to not do what is hard for me to do. When you're committed to taking Massive Action, you naturally have a just-do-it attitude.

Most entrepreneurs I know have a "do it now and ask for forgiveness later" attitude. They forge forward with a just-do-it mentality, figuring things out as they go. They recognize that even if they fail, they will have learned and gained invaluable experience and insight that will help them get it right the next time. Failure allows us to figure out where problems are. Taking quick and Massive Action followed by evaluating results and improving is the way to achieve the quickest results. Sometimes it is the *only* way to achieve results.

Successful people understand this cycle and don't worry about the possibility of initial lack of success. They actually expect it. They recognize that the first time around might be a miserable failure, but they also realize that the quicker they can get through this failure cycle, the quicker they will get to the end result of success. When you stop thinking about possible failure and all the reasons not to take action, you just do it. And when this mindset is a natural part of the way you live your life, you'll find that taking Massive Action—and achieving high-level success—comes naturally.

# CHAPTER 15:
# KEEP THE MOMENTUM

*"You get some momentum going, and anything can happen."*

—Frank Permuy

Take time to understand the concept of momentum, because momentum is critical for Massive Action. In high school physics, we all learned that a body in motion will continue in motion in the same direction until stopped by an opposite action. A snowball rolling down a hill, for example, gains both speed and size as it rolls, and only stops when it hits an obstacle. This is exactly how momentum works in life.

When you first start moving toward something, it might feel like you're trying to roll a huge boulder uphill. If you can get that boulder started, however, momentum and gravity work their magic, and it starts rolling downhill. It takes a lot of energy to get started, but picks up its own strength and speed as it goes.

As you start taking Massive Action, you will experience small wins. Even the thought of moving toward your goal creates energy, excitement, and momentum. Harnessing this initial energy and excitement creates even more momentum. You don't want to waste this initial surge. Many people enjoy mini-victories along the way to success, but they blow it off, saying, "Oh, that was easy. Let's see if this continues before I celebrate too much."

They're doubtful and don't have the rock-solid inner-core belief that they will reach their end goal, so they dismiss small victories and miss the opportunity to harness this initial excitement and power that can lead to greater momentum. You will need this energy when you hit roadblocks. The energy tucked away in reserve can be invaluable. If you dismiss or ignore the energy when it comes—anytime it comes— you will not have it when you need it most. Recognize and celebrate the small victories on your journey of taking Massive Action. No matter how small those victories are, if they move you toward your goal, feel good about it. That feeling is *momentum*, and it only gets bigger and faster if you allow it.

Just as you recognize and celebrate victories along the way, you should also recognize failures along the way. When you realize these failures are part of the process, you diminish the loss of momentum you may experience. Failures become experience; that perspective can prevent failures from destroying the momentum you're gaining.

Every day that you move toward your goal, you gain momentum. There may be stretches, even long ones, when you feel like you're not making progress. If you maintain Massive Action, however, you're moving toward your goal. That's how things work. Few things progress in a linear fashion, with the same amount of movement every day. Success does not work that way. Occasionally you'll have a breakthrough that will launch you to the next level, but just as often, you'll hit a plateau where you'll stay for a while. The important thing is to consistently work hard, even during the plateaus. That consistency will get you the next breakthrough as soon as possible, which will launch you to the next level, which will bring you to the next plateau, which will lead to the next breakthrough. Ultimately, following this process of taking Massive Action leads you to your ultimate goal of success.

Ride the wave of momentum. Don't dismiss it. Momentum will show up if you're working hard and moving forward in your journey.

Be willing to let it in when it knocks on the door. As soon as it shows up, recognize it and use it to your benefit.

I have done this many times. I get into the wrong mind-frame, and even when small things go well, I ignore them, choosing instead to focus on the bad. I don't allow the small wins to start a little momentum. You will have ups and downs. Don't let your downs keep you down; look for the ups, then let them do their job.

Bobby Jones once said, "Golf is the closest game to the game we call life. You get bad breaks from good shots; you get good breaks from bad shots. But you have to play the ball where it lies."[15]

I'm sure you've seen this concept play out in sports on TV. One team might be struggling throughout an entire game, but all it takes is one or two little things to go their way, and all of a sudden, they look like a different team. That spark of momentum carries them to victory.

Successful teams are always looking for that spark of momentum. When they see it, they recognize it immediately and run with it. Unsuccessful teams are the ones that don't believe in momentum or understand the concept. If they're on a losing streak, that's what they focus on. Even when they get a break and a few good things happen, the opportunity disappears into thin air because they didn't recognize that it was momentum knocking on the door. They dismiss it, move on, and lose the game.

This scenario plays out in life too, but over a longer timeframe. No matter who you are, some things *will* go your way. Use the spark of energy those good things create to carry you to success. Believe that you will eventually be successful. Let your rock-solid inner-core belief allow you to look for the little things that can start the momentum train going.

You might have experienced this if you've considered buying a new car. Once you make that decision, you see that car everywhere. Did that make or model just become super popular? Of course not. The same cars have been there all the time, but you started to focus on a specific car, and now you notice it everywhere.

---

15 Brent Beshore, "Golf: The Game of Life," *Forbes*, August 20, 2012, https://www.forbes.com/sites/brentbeshore/2012/08/20/golf-the-game-of-life/#2e132ebf4bcf

Similarly, when you focus on your wins, even the small ones, they will appear everywhere. Ignore them, and they will stay hidden in the shadows. In fact, taking Massive Action allows the sparks of momentum to show up more often and more frequently. Because you're taking action, something good will happen. Because you go to that conference, you might meet that one person who will become your business partner and change your life.

Massive Action creates momentum. When you recognize and celebrate momentum, it creates success. If you squash it, you will stay right where you are.

# CHAPTER 16:
# MAKE IT A LIFESTYLE

*"It's not a diet, it's a lifestyle."*

—Unknown

When you want to get into top physical shape, people will tell you it has to become a lifestyle. For your new behavior to last, it must become part of what you do every day. True change doesn't just last a month or a year—it's something you incorporate into your life. It becomes the new normal. Just like brushing your teeth every day, getting and staying in top physical shape requires a regular schedule of exercise and proper diet for the rest of your life. It's something you get used to and it becomes a habit over time. After a while, you will not be able to live any other way.

The same thought applies to taking Massive Action. It's something you just do—and then it becomes a lifestyle. Whenever you do something new, you should be in the habit of reflexively taking Massive Action. If you have that attitude toward everything in your life, soon you can't imagine living life any other way.

A recent spring break with my kids illustrates what I mean. We started spring break by flying to Orlando on a Friday and working on a crowdfunding campaign for my daughter from Friday through Sunday. The average kid on spring break would be going to camp or playing with friends. My daughter spent her spring break taking a major step toward her dreams. We both did this without thinking much about what "normal" kids would do. It was just part of our lifestyle.

The ultimate goal, of course, is becoming a professional singer-songwriter, but her Massive Action plan includes working on a crowdfunding campaign during spring break. Since Massive Action is my default behavior and lifestyle, I was more excited than anyone else to go to Orlando and start working. I didn't look at it as "missing out" on spring break. I *enjoyed* spring break! I know that Massive Action produces massive results over time, and that gets me more excited than anything.

Some may say that students should take off during spring break, but I disagree. We were spending time together in pursuit of a goal that she set for herself. I'm supporting her 100 percent. She senses that, and it strengthens our relationship. I could not have imagined a better way to start spring break than by taking three days to work on a worthy pursuit that helps my daughter move closer to her dreams.

This is a great example of incorporating Massive Action into your lifestyle. Sure, it falls outside the ordinary spring break experience, but that's what it takes to achieve extraordinary success in life. If your idea of spring break is hanging around on the beach having a good time with friends, you're not taking Massive Action. That mindset is simply not congruent with ultra-success.

While I think it's important to have downtime and recharge your batteries, most people who are into the Massive Action lifestyle would rather be working and getting something done than taking "time off." Those who are into the fitness lifestyle would rather be at the gym, while others cannot comprehend how people can actually enjoy going to the gym. It comes down to what you want in life—the answer to your big *why*.

This boils down to mindset and lifestyle. Once you start taking Massive Action, you realize that being productive and accomplishing something is much more fulfilling than sitting around and taking it easy. The real enjoyment comes from the journey of taking Massive

Action and accomplishing your goals. Those who have achieved physical fitness, for example, are reaping the tremendous rewards of their efforts, and now they would rather be at the gym than just about anywhere else in the world.

Similarly, when you get your mind focused on adopting the Massive Action approach in your lifestyle, you will see tremendous results and want nothing more than to continue your heightened efforts. You will become "outside of ordinary." Ultra-successful people are certainly not the norm in our society; you must be "abnormal" if you want to be successful.

# CHAPTER 17:
# MAKE RAPID DECISIONS

*"Every leader has the courage to make decisions. No decision is usually the worst decision."*

—Orrin Woodward

When you're taking Massive Action, making rapid decisions are part of the process and a necessary skill set. You'll find that successful people, especially entrepreneurs, are rapid decision-makers. People who are unsuccessful and stuck in one place are slow decision-makers.

Of course, rapid decision-making has a downside. As with the swing-big, miss-big mindset, you will miss more than you hit. When you're making rapid decisions, you will get things wrong from time to time. The idea, however, is that over time, you gain more than you lose. And speed is important, because opportunities come and go quickly.

Our reptilian brains instinctively make rapid decisions. Think about any small animal that is prey for another animal. Which is more likely to be eaten—the smart squirrel that thinks things through or the squirrel that is quick and can get away? Evolutionary biology—and your reptilian brain—puts a premium on speed over smarts.

Your reptilian brain processes emotions and wants to act quickly. When the neocortex gets in the way and wants to "think about it," the opportunity often disappears. Remember that the mountain lion eats the squirrel that deliberated.

The casino mentality illustrates this idea. Casinos all over the world make billions of dollars by recognizing the one-percent advantage. Casino owners know they're going to lose 49 percent of the time, but that means they'll win 51 percent of the time. And that's enough to make them billions.

Of course, you don't want to be losing—or making wrong decisions—49 percent of the time, but realistically you might make wrong decisions 10 or 20 percent of the time. You may not even know if a decision is wrong sometimes; sometimes only time will tell. But the point is, it doesn't matter. The experience you gain is invaluable and often can be gained no other way. Remember, even when you're wrong, you'll know better next time. Mistakes are always valuable if you let them teach you something.

When you become a rapid decision-maker, you'll get better and better at it; soon you'll find that you move comfortably at this rapid pace. Your percentage of wrong decisions will go down. It will never reach zero—we all make wrong decisions, regardless of our speed. But you will become so good at rapid decision-making that you move easily at this pace and gain an advantage over those who deliberate excessively.

As an emergency medicine physician for more than 10 years, I know firsthand the importance of making rapid decisions. Life-or-death decisions are routinely made in an ER. I often found myself treating a very ill patient without knowing exactly what was wrong, but I had to act quickly and do my best to prevent a tragic outcome. I couldn't wait for every piece of information—if I did, the patient would likely die. I had to make decisions with the information I had. With experience and time, I got better at making those decisions rapidly.

Colin Powell, a former U.S. Secretary of State, talks about making decisions using the "40-70" rule.[16] He notes that if you have less than 40 percent of the information, you will likely make a wrong decision, while if you wait for more than 70 percent of the information, too often it will be too late and your decision will not matter. We need to make decisions quickly—and often with incomplete data.

Quickly making decisions and taking action is a necessary skill no matter what your profession, and it's an essential part of taking Massive Action. You must understand and accept that some of those decisions will be wrong, and you can't beat yourself up about it. In fact, when things don't work out as you planned and you don't get your desired outcome, you gain something even more valuable—experience. Wrong decisions and failure come with the territory, and if you're not willing to accept this, you'll never be successful.

You know yourself better than anyone. If you think you overanalyze things or take too much time to think about decisions or what people say about you, then you already know you're not making decisions quickly enough. If some people criticize you because you jump into things too quickly, you're probably doing it right. It's just a matter of time before your efforts turn into successes. Making rapid decisions allows you to achieve your goals more quickly, build necessary momentum, and get across the finish line.

---

16  Oren Harari, *The Leadership Secrets of Colin Powell* (New York: McGraw-Hill, 2002).

# CHAPTER 18:
# THE 30-DAY CHALLENGE

*"Thirty days from now you will either be blown away by your results, or blown away by the effort you put in."*

—Sunil Saxena, M.D.

This concept is simple. Whatever you're trying to achieve, whatever habit you're trying to develop, whatever change you want to make, you must do it every day for 30 days.

The 30-day challenge is one of my favorite topics. I have used it so often and so successfully that I am an absolute believer that this is the best way to start taking Massive Action. The same concept could be applied to a seven-day challenge or even a 365-day challenge—any consistent effort made toward accomplishing a goal is called "taking Massive Action." I personally have found that a 30-day challenge seems to be the perfect time frame that creates the momentum I need to continue taking Massive Action until I reach my goal.

I struggled for decades to make going to the gym a regular habit, and I finally used this concept to really get going. I found the 30-day challenge literally life changing. I basically forced myself to go to the gym and follow a predetermined schedule (four different workouts that I rotated every four days) every day for 30 days in a row. I did this right after the blood pressure scare that I talked about earlier.

This structure and short time frame was the catalyst I needed.

First, I made physical gains that I could measure and feel—I was more in shape after 30 days than I had ever been before. This itself made me feel good and added to the momentum I had gained to make going to the gym a part of my regular lifestyle.

Second, I had told my friends and even guys at the gym that I was doing a 30-day challenge, and that helped me stay committed to complete the challenge. I was accountable to others. I got to know trainers and others who were working out at the gym. It was easy to chat with them and report, "Yep, I'm on day 14 of my 30-day challenge." I felt good about what I was doing, and they encouraged me to succeed, even though most of them didn't even know me well.

Third, and most important, the 30-day challenge actually changed my mindset. I think one of my main issues over the years is that I never felt like I was that person who went to the gym. I wasn't a "gym guy." While I had played sports as a child, I never thought of myself as an athlete or someone who was in shape. But after 30 days, I felt like I belonged at the gym; I was an athlete training for an important goal. In my case, the goal was not an athletic performance or competition but rather a desire to live a longer life.

The challenge changed my way of thinking, which is the *most* important benefit of a 30-day challenge. You believe in yourself. You feel like you are that person who should be doing whatever you felt uncomfortable doing before. It pushes you out of your comfort zone and creates a *new* comfort zone. The mental transformation can be remarkable.

I have used the 30-day challenge in other ways, including learning to be more social and going out more. My daughter has used it to overcome stage fright and performing at open-mic events, and my son used it to establish a better golf practice routine. These are just a few examples of how the 30-day challenge can be applied in any area.

When you're starting something new, start with a 30-day challenge. It can be difficult; you might even feel like there is an invisible force trying to stop you. In fact, your body naturally resists doing something new, especially something that takes you out of your comfort zone.

Take just 30 days, even if it means putting other things in your life on hold. You don't have to stop everything, just simplify things so you can devote your time, energy, and willpower to the 30-day challenge. Remember, this is only one month. Your life will not fall apart if you put other things on pause for 30 days. Even if other things suffer a bit, the momentum you gain and the mindset you create to help you achieve your main goals will make the sacrifice worthwhile.

The first 10 days will be the most difficult because you're doing something new, and you need to get used to it. It will get easier toward the end. After 30 days, you'll have established a habit that your body and mind now expect. You'll be programmed to enjoy and look forward to your new routine.

Remarkably, after 30 days I *wanted* to go to the gym. If for some reason I missed a day, I felt like something was wrong. The 30-day challenge was incredibly powerful and launched me on my fitness journey, helping me establish a lifestyle focused on being as healthy as possible.

One of the most important things the challenge did was change my mindset. Prior to the challenge, I had never enjoyed going to the gym, but after 30 days of consistently working out, I now look forward to going. While it's still not one of my favorite activities, I feel like I belong there and enjoy the benefits from being fit.

Whatever massive result you hope to achieve, try the 30-day challenge immediately. Identify a plan, starting *tomorrow*, for whatever you're working on. I'm almost always in the middle of a 30-day challenge for something. It's important, however, to only do one challenge at a time. Once you realize the power of a 30-day challenge, it's enticing to try two or three things at a time because you see the momentum and improvement a successful challenge can create. Doing more than one challenge at a time defeats the entire purpose. All your willpower and strength is required to maintain your 30-day challenge focused on one effort.

Initially, the excitement you feel at making progress can sometimes get you through the first few days of the challenge, or even the first week. Be prepared for that dip that will come at some point. There will be days when massive resistance shows up. It might come early in the challenge or later, but it will invariably come. When it does, don't let it overwhelm you—don't allow your 30-day streak to break. On those days of the dip, you will need all your willpower to push through and get to the end of the 30 days.

Trust me—I've been there. Somewhere between day 10 and day 20, I lose enthusiasm and stop the challenge. In retrospect, I regret it and recognize it wasn't the right choice. But at the time I'm giving up, it makes complete sense. Maybe something important happened, and I convince myself that I have to deal with other things so it's okay to stop. I don't resume the challenge, and soon that particular 30-day challenge is distant memory.

If you've never done something like this, it's hard to explain how powerful this concept can be. A 30-day challenge can get you started on a path to success that you never imaged.

Don't overthink the details—just do it. Start your 30-day challenge today! If you can't build up enough momentum and willpower to sustain the challenge, don't beat yourself up. You at least tried, and you can start again. But if you can stick to a 30-day challenge no matter what, it will change your life.

# CHAPTER 19:
# DEVELOP MINI HABITS

*"It's not what we do once in a while that shapes our lives, it's what we do consistently."*[17]

—Tony Robbins

When you are taking Massive Action, understanding the concept of mini habits can be the difference between success and failure. Stephen Guise explains this beautiful idea in his book, *Mini Habits: Smaller Habits, Bigger Results.*[18] The basic concept is to break your actions down into the smallest incredibly easy thing you can do. The idea of mini habits was life changing for me, and I recommend reading this book completely and adding it to your tool set.

The 30-day challenge I explained in Chapter 19 works well with this concept. Mini habits can keep you on track during the rough times. They can work in conjunction with your 30-day challenge or any other sustained effort that takes you outside your comfort zone and requires tremendous willpower.

---

17 Tony Robbins, *Awaken the Giant Within* (New York: Free Press, 1991).
18 Stephen Guise, *Mini Habits: Smaller Habits, Bigger Results* (CreateSpace, 2013).

When we're taking Massive Action, an invisible force works to stop us dead in our tracks. (See Chapter 36.) We want to move forward on a conscious level, but this force keeps us from doing what we know we should be—and often *want* to be—doing. Whether it's a mental, physical, or emotional issue we are facing, we find reasons to justify why we're not doing what we know is best for us.

When I first started getting into shape, it took me years to get the habit down consistently. Even though I went to the gym for a few weeks, or even a few months, eventually I would stop. I knew going to the gym was in my best interest, especially in the long term. The problem, however, is that that negative force showed up and prevented me from continuing.

The invisible force can take many different shapes. Maybe you start thinking your goal isn't important enough, or you're too busy, or you're too tired, or you're just not making enough gains to justify the effort. This force showed up in my life for many years, preventing me from making permanent changes.

Mini habits can be a powerful way to develop momentum and overcome this force. For example, if you're struggling to get to the gym regularly and you set a goal of going to the gym four times a week, maybe your mini habit would be to show up at the gym and do one push-up. Something so incredibly simple it sounds stupid—but it works. Even just walking into the gym and walking back out could by your minimum mini habit that allows you to declare success.

First, going to the gym four times a week needs to become a physical habit. Sometimes just getting there can be the barrier. If the gym is not nearby (more than 15 minutes' travel time), the force to prevent you can be strong. If it's winter and cold and dark outside, your body does not want to get up. Then your mind starts thinking about how much time it's going to take just to get there and back. Those thoughts can derail the entire train you're trying to get rolling.

If you develop a mini habit of doing just a little workout, it's easier to tell yourself how easy it would be to just get up, do a few weights or cardio, and then come back. The result, of course, will be that you will end up doing more than that. In fact, by the time you get to the gym, you'll be awake and much more physically and mentally ready to complete a full workout.

I've used this concept over and over in life, and it can be the key to success when you're encountering the type of force that prevents you from doing things. Mini habits can be the trick to get you going and build needed momentum. Momentum—no matter how small—is still momentum, and it will snowball and get bigger and bigger until you're taking Massive Action without even thinking about it.

## CHAPTER 20:
# SET A SCHEDULE

*"Successful people are simply those with successful habits."*
—Brian Tracy[19]

Once you've established some mini habits, it's important to set a schedule and keep developing productive habits. When you first begin to take Massive Action in any area, it can be difficult. Remember that as you move forward, things become easier and easier. This is where habits take over.

Imagine driving from your house to work every day. Perhaps initially it was difficult because you didn't know the route. Over time, however, you find you can actually drive almost subconsciously; you don't even think about it. Often you'll show up at work and not even remember driving there. You've created such a habit that your subconscious mind has taken over and done the task for you. This frees up your conscious mind to do other things, such as brainstorming about an upcoming project or listening intently to an audio book.

This is why habits are so efficient: they allow you to multitask. A

---

19  Brian Tracy, Facebook page, October 6, 2011, https://www.facebook.com/BrianTracyPage/posts/10150318238643460.

habit allows you to transfer tasks from your conscious mind to your subconscious, freeing up your conscious mind to do other things. It's like putting your car on autopilot—you don't have to worry about sticking to the speed limit once you've set the control; you can focus on keeping an eye out for erratic drivers instead.

Similarly, when you're taking Massive Action, you'll eventually reach the point where certain things become habits, and your subconscious takes over. This allows your mental bandwidth the freedom and ability to do increasingly more things. It's important to be aware of the concept that initially things can seem difficult, but over time habits form and things become significantly easier.

This is where the concept of the 30-day challenge is so critical. After a month, you'll have formed a new habit, or at least be very close to it. Your subconscious mind can then take over and do a lot of things for you while you focus on bigger and better things.

One specific area that is essential is establishing a morning routine. When I have a set routine from the moment I wake up, I'm much more productive during the day. When my morning routine slips, I become less focused and disciplined about accomplishing things. When Daylight Savings Time changes my schedule, for example, I find myself doing more in the evening. I stay up later . . . and, naturally, get up later. This year when the clocks all sprang forward, I was unproductive for the first few days of the new schedule. I didn't know why, until I realized that my morning routine had gone off track. I immediately forced myself to get back on the routine, and sure enough, my productivity went up to what I would normally expect.

Hal Elrod wrote a great book, *Miracle Morning*, about the value of a morning routine. It's another must-read book for anybody who wants to take Massive Action and be extremely successful. He outlines the concept of starting your day properly and offers suggestions on how to do this. It's such an important concept that it deserves to be the subject of an entire book. I highly recommend reading and studying it.

Setting a schedule and developing habits is so important. Make sure you understand the concept, and push yourself to do it. A habit can be formed in 30 to 60 days—in the grand scheme of things, that's a very short time compared to the huge benefit you'll receive. It's worth taking the time to do this systematically, because these habits will serve you tremendously for the rest of your life. They will help you achieve a level of success you may not have thought was possible.

# CHAPTER 21:
# OVERWHELM YOUR OTHER SENSES

*"If you overthink things, practice turning it off—and watch the magic happen."*

—Sunil Saxena, M.D.

Often when you're trying to take Massive Action, your fear and other emotions will hold you back. Interestingly, dogs and babies don't have emotions that get in the way—they just react spontaneously. In most situations, they simply do what they want to do. That's why they always "steal the show." While this may not always be the right behavior for an adult, thinking a little less and doing a little more can be much-needed medicine for adults in many situations. Most of us overthink things.

A benefit of taking Massive Action is that you actually overcome your senses. It's an interesting phenomenon and one that you can use to your advantage.

Think of the last time you really enjoyed yourself in a social situation. Likely you were in a comfortable environment with great friends, or maybe you were just in a great mood. You were calm and free and having a fun time. Not a lot of thinking, just living in the moment.

You may not have realized it, but you were not allowing your senses to block you in that situation. You weren't thinking about what people might be thinking of you; you were not wondering if they liked you. You weren't thinking about why you were there, you didn't want to go home, you weren't worried about what to say next, and you weren't concerned whether it was the "right" thing to say. You were just being you. Your authenticity came out, and that's what makes you so attractive to others—and increases your self-confidence.

The same thing happens when you're taking Massive Action. Focusing all your efforts on achieving your goals brings out the real you and increases your confidence; your other senses, the ones that make you hesitate and overthink a situation, don't get in the way. Taking Massive Action allows you to put the overly analytical part of your brain aside and just keep going. More importantly, it doesn't stop your momentum!

One of the most interesting things about working in the emergency room is the swift pace. I've heard someone say that the average ER doctor makes over 2,000 decisions in a 10-hour shift. Sometimes it felt like even more! I remember times when I had to go to the bathroom so bad I felt like I couldn't hold it anymore—but six hours later, I realized I still hadn't gone.

In certain high-pressure situations, when it feels like so much is being thrown at you so quickly, many of your senses simply turn off so you can focus and get things done. Sometimes the pressure is so intense that it actually turns off the physical trigger in your brain that tells you it's time to urinate. It also relaxes your bladder so it can accommodate more volume and reduces the urge to pee.

On a larger scale, this is the same phenomenon that often accompanies taking Massive Action. As you focus intensely on working toward your goals, you can block unwanted thoughts and even impulses that would fight against your progress. Overwhelming your other senses can happen in fits and starts as you take Massive Action and find yourself in the zone. This allows you to advance to the next level. Sometimes you lose your rhythm and revert back to a state where you are overthinking things. It's definitely an up-and-down cycle. Just remember that wherever you are in that cycle, if you push through and continue to take Massive Action, your momentum will get going again. The more times you go through this cycle, the longer the zone will last and the quicker you can get back into the right zone.

# CHAPTER 22:
# GO BACK TO BASICS

*"Simplicity boils down to two steps: identify the essentials, eliminate the rest."*

—Leo Babauta[20]

Often when taking Massive Action, people need to go back to the basics. Nothing I talk about in this book is complicated, but if you are feeling that it is, think about the basics. As with most things that lead to success in life, what I'm talking about is simple but not easy. Lou Holtz put it perfectly when he noted that, when you're trying to establish goals, there are just six things to consider. Holtz says to answer the following six questions honestly:

1. What sacrifice will I make?
2. What am I willing to pay?
3. What skills or talents do I need?
4. Who do you have to work with?

---

20 Leo Babauta, *The Power of Less: The Fine Art of Limiting Yourself to the Essential . . . in Business and in Life* (New York: Hachette Books, 2008).

5. What problems and obstacles are you going to have to overcome?

6. What's your plan?[21]

Vince Lombardi, the greatest coach in NFL history, said that games are decided by the basics. He famously said, "Some people try to find things in this game that do not exist, but football is only two things—blocking and tackling."[22] Whoever blocks and tackles better will win the game. When we analyze modern sports, we often overlook these fundamentals.

The same holds true in golf. Amateurs often struggle and cannot figure out the game. They use technology to look at ball flight, swing speed, swing path, club face, and more. But the solution is found in the basics— your grip, the set up, and your weight distribution at address. It's the basics that almost nobody ever practices.

Jack Nicklaus, one of the greatest golfers of all time, said he started each practice session with a review of the basics. The advanced stuff is important as well, but he never forgot the basics.

The top-level pros in all sports review the fundamentals on a daily basis to make sure that nothing is "off." In golf, even being off an eighth of an inch can mean the difference between hitting the ball into a water hazard or getting a hole in one. It's the same in life. If you fail to review the basics and are just a little bit off in a certain area, it can have a dramatic impact as you're taking Massive Action and moving forward.

It's amazing how many people move past the basics because they're worried about the advanced stuff. They figure that the journey has to be hard and complicated. If it were simple, everyone would be successful, right? So they look for complex answers, instead of focusing on the basics.

If you master the basics and check on them regularly to make sure they're consistent, you will build a solid foundation on which you can add advanced skills and knowledge. Don't overthink it. Simplify and get back to fundamentals!

---

21 Steve Borek, "Six Questions to Ask Yourself to Achieve Your Goals," *Endgame Business*, September 11, 2015, http://endgamebusiness.com/six-questions-to-ask-yourself-to-achieve-your-goals/.

22 Ann Kannings, *Vince Lombardi: His Words* (Raleigh, NC: Lulu Press, 2014).

# CHAPTER 23:
# REMOVE FEAR

*"Thinking will not overcome fear, but action will."*
—W. Clement Stone

The English language should have a new four-letter curse word that starts with F: fear. This four-letter word has caused many people to miss out on great opportunities, experiences, and successes in their lives.

*Wreck-It Ralph* fans will remember what Calhoun said about it:

"'Fear' is a four-letter word, ladies. You wanna go pee-pee in your big-boy slacks, keep it to yourself! It's make-your-mama-proud time!"

Fear is something we are genetically programmed with. If you've studied evolutionary biology, you understand that having fear is an essential part of our survival mechanism. Ten thousand years ago, our fear was calibrated and developed to a perfect level that allowed us to survive. Millennia ago, humans were right to be afraid of many things. A simple disease could kill you, and there were always hungry wild animals lurking about. When Mother Nature became especially difficult during winter, you could die. This was the reality that the world we lived in until the last hundred years or so.

Today, however, most of the things our ancestors feared wouldn't really have any impact on our life. With modern technology, medicine, and society, the most serious things that kill us are self-inflicted. We don't have to be afraid of a tiger killing us. Natural disasters, while they happen, are less destructive than ever. And while some diseases are still dreaded, many are controlled and cured. What you should really fear is the lack of knowledge and self-awareness that can sabotage your Massive Action.

The problem is that our brain's operating system is 10,000 years old. Too much has happened to the human race in a relatively short amount of time, making it difficult for our innate biology to adapt. The good news is that we are conscious beings, and we can consciously achieve this type of adaptation. It's not easy, but with hard work, it can certainly be done.

Fear is often referred to as "False Evidence Appearing Real." The key word is *false*. We don't have to be afraid of 99 percent of the things that our outdated genetic programming tells us we should fear.

The majority of people I meet are afraid of public speaking. I can relate—I felt that same fear until I spoke so many times that it became no big deal. Can you imagine getting up in front of your tribe 10,000 years ago? If you said or did something they didn't like, there's a good chance you might be killed, especially if the leader of the tribe was angered. That is why the fear of public speaking is equivalent to the fear of death for some people. It's amazing how powerful this fear can be. Public speaking evokes the same fight-or-flight response as coming face to face with a hungry tiger that thinks you are dinner.

Of course, the worst thing that could happen if you speak publicly in front of a group of people today is that you might say or do something that would cause incredible embarrassment. You wouldn't die, and I doubt anybody would even remember what happened a day later. You might just end up with a bruised ego.

In the mid-20$^{th}$ century, Moe Norman was an exceptionally talented golfer. He apparently had a form of mild autism, likely Asperger's Syndrome, although it was not diagnosed at that time. He was extremely uncomfortable around strangers and did not like social situations. He repeatedly found himself in positions to win tournaments; he often had a huge lead with only three or four holes left. Time after time, however, he would blow his lead, and another golfer would win. Many people surmised that it was because Moe didn't want to endure the trophy ceremony. His fear of engaging with strangers actually caused him to lose golf tournaments.

Imagine working so hard and being in a position to win golf tournaments easily, yet not wanting to win because you were afraid of speaking in public! It's hard to imagine sitting on the sidelines and watching Moe do that, but the reality is that we have all probably experienced similar situations where we have sabotaged something because of fear. Maybe we don't do it purposefully—and Moe probably didn't either. But if our subconscious mind is fearful, that affects our conscious mind and our actions.

While Moe is an extreme case, it does illustrate that we are often our own cause of failure. We frequently push away the very success we crave. I tell my children that in our modern society, 80 percent of the bad things that happen to us are self-inflicted. When I review my life and my failures, I can directly link at least 80 percent of them to my own actions.

I'm sure you've experienced this in your life to some extent. Often people don't feel worthy of the success. They don't feel like it could happen to them. They feel like they're a fake or an imposter—a poser. But if you put in the hard work and sacrifice and dedicate yourself to your goal, you deserve every ounce of success you earn. Someone has to get the prize; why not you?

If you find yourself falling in this trap, determine whether you're afraid of success or whether you feel unworthy of success. If you struggle with these issues, it's important to take Massive Action to fix them before you take on the challenge of moving toward your high-level goals. If you're going to sabotage yourself in the end because you're afraid, there's no point in making the effort. Feeling worthy is a foundation for success. Do whatever it takes for you to personally feel worthy of the success.

Fear is probably the number-one reason that stops people from taking Massive Action. They're simply afraid of what might happen. I could share one example after another of situations where people have not taken action because they were afraid of an unlikely outcome.

Understanding fear and where it's coming from can help.

Whenever you feel fear, recognize it and think, "Oh, there it is again." Acknowledge it, but then dismiss it. Remind yourself that fear is typically completely unfounded, and nothing bad will happen. While this can be difficult, with practice you can overcome fear.

Dive head first into the things you're most afraid of. This will teach your brain that you're not going to give into fear and that you are determined to overcome, no matter what. Whatever you're most afraid of is the exact thing you should be undertaking. Even if it has nothing to do with your primary goals, take it on. This will teach your brain that fear won't get in your way of success.

Take inventory of your fears. Fear can take many forms, and as conscious beings, we don't always want to admit that fear is what is stopping us. We often make up other reasons for not doing something, but fear is usually the underlying reason for our choices and behavior. Once you have practiced overcoming fear in one area, use that same experience to deal with fear in other areas. It will get easier each time you confront fear.

# CHAPTER 24:
# USE FEAR OF MISSING OUT (FOMO)

*"Don't fear FOMO. Use it to your advantage."*
—Sunil Saxena, M.D.

One fear, however, can be useful. Fear of missing out—or FOMO, as the kids call it—is a powerful motivating tool that can support you as you take Massive Action. Typically, FOMO is viewed as a bad or negative thing. You can turn this around and use it to your advantage.

Keep reminding yourself of all the incredible opportunities you have and the great things that will happen to you if you take Massive Action. Think of all the great things you're missing out on by not accomplishing your goals. Those thoughts can continue to motivate you and push you through what is stopping you.

Most of us realize that we only have a certain time on this earth. Remind yourself that you only have one life, one chance to take Massive Action that will lead to these things. This is not a dress rehearsal—make this life what you want it to be *now*. Don't waste your opportunities!

For me this has specifically helped with my social life. I typically take Massive Action all day regarding my business goals. In the evening, I like to go out and work on my social skills and life. However, I am often tired at the end of the day and skip my planned evening activities. Once I started to remind myself of all of the great personal and professional relationships I was missing out on by skipping my planned evening activities, I was motivated to look forward to these activities and not skip them. I look back and evaluate all the great relationships I have developed over the years in a social setting. I use this as fuel to develop FOMO and continue to stay consistent with my evening plans. It's a powerful technique that has worked for me, and I know it can work for you.

A vision board can also be a powerful tool to develop FOMO. Cut out pictures of things you want to accomplish, and stick them up on a board that you look at every day. Place it strategically so that you will naturally see it regularly throughout the day, perhaps at your desk or office where you spend a lot of time. When you look at the board, think about missing out on all these great things. I have used the vision-board technique many times to great success. I envision in great detail what I want, and I play the movie over and over in my head. I keep reminding myself that if I don't take Massive Action and work hard, I will miss out on all these great things. A vision board can provide that critical spark of motivation during your down periods throughout the day.

Time is our most precious asset—use it wisely. We must be in a continuous state of taking Massive Action if we want to have the kind of life we've dreamed of. Make FOMO your friend, and use it as a great motivational tool that encourages and reminds you to take Massive Action. As each day progresses, play the movie over and over in your head of the goals you want to achieve. Maintain a healthy fear of missing out on these things, and let that fear motivate you to get the job done.

# CHAPTER 25:
# DON'T TAKE ACTION FOR ACTION'S SAKE

*"I don't think action for action's sake is so fun, but when it helps tell the story, I love a good fight scene."*
—Joseph Gordon-Levitt[23]

I've placed a great emphasis on taking action in this book, but here's a word of caution: don't take action just for action's sake. You see people who do this—they're extremely busy but don't seem to be accomplishing anything. People fall into this trap for myriad reasons. Maybe they're insecure and want to look important. Maybe they fear success, or perhaps they cannot truly believe that they can be successful or are worthy of success. Or maybe deep down they don't really want what they say they want. Whatever the case, I see people who insist they are "busy" but are merely spinning their wheels like a hamster—never going anywhere.

---

23  Becky Kirsch, "Joseph Gordon-Levitt and Emily Blunt Talk Looper and Bruce Willis Imitations," July 13, 2012, https://www.popsugar.com/entertainment/Joseph-Gordon-Levitt-Looper-Prosthetics-23981489.

I know I fall into this trap easily myself. I am the type of person who enjoys being busy. At the end of the day if I've accomplished a lot and checked things off my list, I feel good. I enjoy that feeling. The only problem is that the list could be filled with things that either did not need to be done by me or are not in line with my high-level goals. I'm the type of person who likes to "work hard." The key is not just hard work in and of itself but making sure that the hard work is aligned with your long-term goals and your *why*.

I've worked very hard in my life, but often it was because I enjoyed being a "busy beaver." I've also put in a lot of hard work that wasn't in line with my *why*. Don't fall into this trap. Don't take action just for action's sake.

There is no virtue in being busy. What matters are your results.

The psychology can be complex. Many individuals who are typical busy beavers—always running around breathlessly with a list a mile long—simply feel better about themselves when say they have a hectic schedule. They're accomplishing something; they're checking off boxes on their to-do lists. Sometimes they'll add something new to their list after they've done it, just to have one more thing to check off. They are often hiding a deep insecurity that their lives aren't significant and they don't feel worthy of true success.

This concept is similar to the perfect practice concept in sports. I often see people hitting balls endlessly at the golf driving range with the wrong technique. They are taking Massive Action, but that action is not aligned with their long-term goal of becoming a better golfer. If anything, it is making them worse since it is reinforcing the wrong swing. It is practicing (or taking Massive Action) to fix specific issues in your swing that make you a better golfer not just endlessly hitting balls. Be sure you are working towards specific goals and taking Massive Action in a deliberate direction and not just taking action to feel busy.

Make sure that if you're taking Massive Action, you're actually moving towards supporting your long-term vision of the higher goals that you set for yourself and not just spinning your wheels.

# CHAPTER 26:
# SET S.M.A.R.T. GOALS

*"Setting goals is the first step in turning the invisible into the visible."*

—Unknown

One of the best ways to ensure that you are directing your efforts properly toward your end goal is to establish S.M.A.R.T. goals. The original concept for this acronym comes from George T. Doran in his 1981 paper, "There's a S.M.A.R.T. Way to Write Management's Goals and Objectives," but I have my own definition:

## S: SPECIFIC

When you're setting goals, make sure they are specific. Understand your end result clearly. You must know what you're specifically trying to accomplish so you can measure if you're successful or not.

For example, if you want to be a better golfer and set that as your goal, you'll find it difficult to measure. The goal is vague and undefined. What does it mean to be "a better golfer"? There's room for a lot of interpretation; it's too subjective.

Set a more specific goal, such as shooting a 75 average over 10 rounds or driving the ball 280 yards with 70 percent of fairways hit. That's a specific goal that is easy to measure.

If your driver improves, then your overall score will improve, and you will, indeed, become a better golfer. You can measure the driver goal, which is a key component of becoming a better golfer. This becomes your component goal: a measurable goal that contributes to your overall goal, which may not be as measurable.

## M: MEASURABLE

When you have specific goals, they are easy to measure. You cannot gauge improvement if you cannot measure what you're doing. So your first step is to measure where you are now, then evaluate where you want to be and how you can improve.

Imagine an Olympic athlete trying to run faster—but not clocking her times. How would she know if she's getting faster? You must measure where you are starting from so you can tell if you're improving. When you measure something, you establish a benchmark and can gauge your progress.

My son, the aspiring golfer, is currently working on his iron play. We just came off a winter season where he worked on getting his swing mechanics as technically sound as possible. (The kid has a pretty mean swing.) He had been feeling frustrated because he wasn't making much progress hitting the irons well. We started to measure the variables in his golf swing, and it became clear that his path was way too right; 13 degrees, for you golfers out there. We worked on it, continued to measure, then worked on it some more. Now his path is close to zero degrees, exactly where we want it. And—no surprise—he is now hitting his irons beautifully. Because we measured, we were able to fix the problem. If we hadn't measured, he would still be struggling and frustrated.

## A: ACHIEVABLE

Whenever you're setting goals, make sure they are achievable. This can be difficult, because it's also important not to limit your dreams and aspirations. And we're not talking about setting limits here, although people do tend to get confused about the difference. I want you to dream as big as possible, but when you're setting goals, you may need to back it down and chunk out the steps on your path to the bigger goal.

For example, if I want to be an astronaut, I should never put any limits on what I can ultimately achieve. However, if I put that as my goal right now, I'm setting myself up for failure because it's unrealistic.

A more practical approach is to look at all the requirements for becoming an astronaut and pick one to start working on. That is a smaller, achievable goal that supports my larger goal and is more attainable in my current situation. (Disclaimer: I have never been an astronaut and have no desire to become one.)

Give your mind something it can wrap itself around. The human brain is an amazing creation, and once you start feeding it with certain thoughts and goals, it automatically moves toward those goals without you even consciously knowing it. The brain must feel the goals are attainable, however; your subconscious mind can be smarter than the conscious you sometimes. If your brain feels the goal is unattainable, it will start rejecting it, and you will struggle to stay motivated. Your brain basically says, "Yeah, whatever. Good luck with that." (Yes, your subconscious can be sarcastic.)

You must give your brain something it can realistically accept and work with. As long as your goals are within the realm of reason and you feel confident that they are attainable, then both your conscious and subconscious mind will work together to achieve the goal. Once you attain the current goal, then move on to the next one, which also has to be attainable within your skill set at the time.

This is called "chunking." Take a larger goal and break it down into smaller attainable goals, or chunks. Eventually you will reach your larger goal as long as you keep moving forward on the smaller chunks.

# R: RELEVANT

This is one of the most overlooked parts of a S.M.A.R.T. goal. Take this seriously and make sure that the goal you've chosen is relevant. In other words, will the goal actually support your long-term vision? We often think something will help us so we work hard to achieve it, only to find out afterward that it didn't support our long-term vision.

You'll find many examples of this. For me, going to medical school was one such irrelevant goal. I was young when I started the program, and in my mind, it was an important goal to accomplish. Although it was a goal that my parents had at least partially established, I also felt it would be a good thing for my long-term future. However, I didn't really think about whether being a doctor fit with my own long-term lifestyle vision. It sounded good at the time, so I just did it.

Once you get into something like medical training, you get so busy it's hard to find time to think about your goals and real purpose in life. You simply focus on getting through the program and graduating. I woke up almost a decade later and realized that being a doctor wasn't what I wanted to do with my life. It's not that I was unhappy being a doctor; it just wasn't what made me truly happy.

Today, I'm supporting my daughter with her vision of being a singer-songwriter. I see artists all the time who have identified a goal of recording an album or signing a deal with a record label. What they don't realize is that neither of these goals will necessarily make them "successful"—unless their end goal stops with recording an album or signing a deal. Once you have an album, then what? How are you going to market the album? How are you going to get people to listen? Who's your target audience? All those questions need to be thought through even before the album is put together.

Similarly, getting a record deal doesn't ensure success either. In fact, most people who get a record deal end up being unsuccessful, at least monetarily. You still must have a mechanism in place to get people to listen to your music. Musicians forget that, at the end of the day, music is a business just like any other, and you must get customers in the door. In this case, "customers" means fans who listen to your music. If you don't have a mechanism for that to happen, all the other goals you set will be unsuccessful.

## T: TIMEFRAME

All goals need a timeframe. People often try to argue with me on this, but this point is crucial. Even if you don't achieve the goal within the timeframe, you can reset and re-establish a new timeframe. Make sure to put the timeframe in writing so you can refer back and know when each goal is scheduled to be completed.

Parkinson's Law states that the time it takes to accomplish a task will expand to the time allotted. With that in mind, set a realistic deadline with consequences, or you'll put things off forever. If the goal does not have a timeline, it most likely will never get done. Remember the last time you were leaving for vacation? I bet you got a lot done that day as you prepared to leave!

A timeframe focuses your subconscious brain on a deadline when things must happen. It forces you to work harder, smarter, and quicker. If you don't accomplish a goal in the allotted timeframe, you can analyze the situation and identify what went wrong. Was the timeframe too short? Or was the implementation of the goal faulty? Timelines give you a specific date to aim for, then allow you to re-evaluate and improve.

There's nothing magic about the dates. Your timeframe can be a day, a week, a month, a year, or any other period.

Always use the S.M.A.R.T. principles as a checklist when you set goals. Being disciplined and ensuring each goal meets the checklist above will determine your success or failure. If you don't use this acronym as an outline, you will likely miss something important and invest a lot of time and effort that don't pay off in the long run.

# CHAPTER 27:
# REVIEW HIGH-LEVEL GOALS DAILY

*"A goal is a dream with a deadline."*

—Napoleon Hill[24]

One important thing to do when taking Massive Action is to review your high-level goals daily. My high-level goals are on my phone, and I look at them within the first hour of waking up as part of my morning routine. I also review my *why* statement on a daily basis, which keeps me on track at a high level. This puts me in the right frame of mind for the day and reminds me why I am doing what I do. It reminds me of the eventual outcome I want. It helps my subconscious and conscious mind work together instead of fighting each other, and it helps my emotions relax and allows me to be at optimal productivity during the day.

When things aren't going right, reviewing your high-level goals daily reminds you why you're doing what you're doing and has a calming effect when you realize you're moving towards your ultimate goals.

---

24  Barry J. Farber, *Diamond Power: Gems of Wisdom from America's Greatest Marketer* (Wayne, NJ: Career Press, 2004).

When you take Massive Action, things can become chaotic, and it's easy to get distracted by focusing on checking off day-to-day tasks. Those daily tasks are important, but keeping high-level goals constantly in mind keeps things orderly.

Checking your high-level goals daily also helps ensure that you are doing something every day to help you achieve those big goals. It ensures you're taking Massive Action in the right area. When you get caught up in day-to-day tasks that don't affect your long-term goals, you may feel like you're taking Massive Action when in reality, you're not actually moving toward your goals.

It's similar to driving a car in a straight line or in a circle. If you're taking Massive Action that isn't in line with your goals, you're just driving in a circle and won't ever arrive anywhere. Make sure that at least part of every day, you're taking Massive Action that moves you toward your high-level goals.

When you review your goals first thing in the morning, you can make sure that the planned effort for the day is in line with those goals as much as possible. You have an opportunity to evaluate whether your time is wasted on things you think have to get done (daily chores) but don't move you toward your higher-level goals. This gives you the opportunity to re-evaluate those tasks.

Remember, the point of taking Massive Action is to achieve your high-level goals. That's why we work hard and do what we do. If we're not moving towards high-level goals, then our efforts are wasted. Our daily review makes sure we're not getting off track. When a pilot flies an aircraft, he is constantly reviewing the altitude and direction of the plane to ensure that the plane is taking the most direct route to its destination. Reviewing your high-level goals at least daily accomplishes the same purpose.

Reviewing your high-level goals before you go to bed is also a powerful concept. This helps your subconscious mind even more as it works to provide solutions and direction while you're sleeping. When you wake up in the morning, you'll be even better prepared to plan the day and make sure you're using as much of your day as possible to work toward these goals.

# CHAPTER 28:
# ELIMINATE AND OUTSOURCE

*"The ability to simplify means to eliminate the unnecessary so that the necessary may speak."*

—Hans Hofman[25]

One of the main topics we've discussed as you take Massive Action is making sure that your efforts are directed towards the high-level goals you want to achieve. Life has a way of distracting us, making us focus on day-to-day minutia that doesn't get us anywhere. If, like me, you suddenly realize 10 years have passed and you feel like you haven't achieved your maximum potential, this is likely why.

Sometimes you focus daily on what you think must get done and what you feel is important. Over time, however, you begin to realize that some things don't matter, and you realize how important it is to focus on your high-level goals. One way to do this is to outsource non-essential tasks and eliminate as much from your plate as possible.

When my kids were growing up, we had nannies. While this was an expensive option, it was amazing how much it helped me focus on other things. I accomplished so much more because I didn't have to

---

[25] Jay Sankey, *Zen and the Art of Stand-Up Comedy* (New York: Routledge, 1998).

worry about picking up the kids from school or taking them to activities and other things that didn't require my presence. I played Mr. Mom several times, and I can attest that it was much more difficult to get things done.

Having nannies actually helped me spend more quality time with my children. I was not as tired with the day-to-day tasks that come with raising children: cleaning, cooking, shopping, laundry, and so on. I didn't get frustrated with them as easily and was in the right state when I was spending time with them. I could focus on their goals and help them achieve success. I wasn't worried about chores or errands. These things are a necessary part of providing proper care for children, but it's nice when you can spend quality time with your children and focus on the important aspects of their life.

You can outsource many things relatively inexpensively, including mowing the lawn, cleaning the house, and doing laundry. Online purchasing on websites such as Amazon.com can be a lifesaver. I typically buy 90 percent of all my items online with a click of a button. It's much simpler and saves time—compared to physically driving to a store and spending a good chunk of the day running errands. I buy almost everything online, including my last two cars (not from Amazon).

Evaluate your life and take inventory of everything you do on a daily basis. Maybe even write a list of your responsibilities for one week. Write down everything you do on an hourly basis. Once you have this weekly inventory, go through it and identify things you can outsource.

This powerful technique frees up time so that you can focus on taking Massive Action directed toward your goals. When you eliminate the day-to-day tasks that can be outsourced, you'll be amazed how much time you can free up to actually move forward with your objectives.

As you become more successful, you can outsource more and more. When you get stuck in a cycle of doing the tasks that do not allow you to be successful and grow, you'll never gain the mental or financial ability to outsource more and more non-essential tasks.

Adopt this mantra: outsource, outsource, outsource. If someone else can perform a service at a reasonable cost, outsource the job! Your time is valuable, and when you're taking Massive Action, you need to direct most of your time toward your high-level goals. When you're stuck doing day-to-day tasks, you'll have a hard time moving forward.

# CHAPTER 29:
# BLOCK UNINTERRUPTED TIME

*"Until we can manage time, we can manage nothing else."*

—Peter Drucker

Another important aspect of taking Massive Action is to block uninterrupted time. Everyone's circumstances are different, but having a block of time in the morning and afternoon with no interruptions can help you accomplish your goals.

We've all had those days when we've planned to get something done within a certain time frame, and it just doesn't happen. A task should take about three hours . . . but three hours later, it's still not done. You started off with good intentions, but then various disruptions (I call them "pattern interrupts") derail your plans. Other people might interrupt you, or a personal demand gets in the way. These things distract you, and three days later, you're wondering why you didn't accomplish what you set out to do.

This is a dangerous pitfall you must avoid. In order to take Massive Action toward your high-level goals, you need time blocks where you can focus and not be interrupted. It's an absolute must. Block out uninterrupted time, and then make sure that nothing but an absolute emergency interrupts you. Find a way to make it happen.

Even if you have to schedule this time in the evenings or weekends, that's the way it has to be. If you don't, you'll be stuck right where you are, and you won't make progress on high-level goals.

Our schedules and personal demands vary, so figure out what works best for you. Maybe it's an early-morning slot from 5 to 8, before others wake up. Maybe you have blocks during the day at strategic times. Maybe it's only evenings and weekends. Whatever it is, do what it takes to allow time to take the Massive Action that leads to massive results.

I recommend a minimum of two-hour blocks; it takes that long to get things going and get into the flow of doing something. Three- or four-hour blocks are ideal. Schedule them on your calendar, and have them repeat on a weekly basis, so they become a habit. Schedule them at least a day earlier, so when you wake up you can hit the ground running. Know when your uninterrupted time is and what needs to happen in those blocks. Don't let anyone or anything get in the way of being productive during those times!

## CHAPTER 30:
# USE A HIGH-LEVEL STRATEGY

*"Hope is not a strategy."*

—Rudy Giuliani[26]

When taking Massive Action, you need a high-level strategy, one that takes a 30,000-foot view of your life. Start by looking at every area of your life, including business, finances, friends, family, recreation, spirituality, and anything else that is important to you. Remember to consider what you want in *all* areas of your life—see the big picture. Overly focusing on one area leads to imbalance and diminishes long-term happiness.

One of the important things I learned while building various businesses is that defining what you want is important. What is your big *why*? While taking Massive Action, it is easy to over-focus in one area. Focus is essential to accomplishing goals, but having a high-level plan in place and checking progress along your journey ensures that everything fits together with your overall long-term vision. Your

---

26 Comments at National Republican Convention, St. Paul, Minnesota, September 3, 2008.

business (if you have one) should support your lifestyle, not the other way around.

At times while taking Massive Action, your life may become unbalanced. Sometimes this is necessary for a few months or even a few years to accomplish a specific goal. This is okay as long as you do not lose sight of the big picture and have a plan to bring back the balance as soon as possible.

In my late 20s, I got involved with a restaurant business for about two years. I quickly realized it put a tremendous strain on my lifestyle. Restaurants are challenging businesses that essentially operate 24/7. I realize most restaurants aren't open around the clock, but they might as well be. While owning a restaurant can be financially rewarding, it's also extremely taxing and is definitely not the right lifestyle for everyone. While I enjoyed the idea of owning restaurants, I now know it wasn't the right lifestyle for me.

What I truly desired, although I didn't know it at the time, was a business that provided me with freedom from both location and time constraints. I don't want a business that ties me down to a fixed location or schedule. This might not rank high on a list of priorities for others, but it's important to me. So when I'm examining my high-level goals, I keep that aspect in mind as I decide on the right overall plan of action.

You can achieve a lifestyle that provides all the aspects you want as long as you identify a high-level strategy up front and understand exactly what you want. How will your business or financial endeavors interact with your personal and family life? How will that affect your time to have fun and enjoy life? Take the time to figure out a high-level strategy based on answers to these types of questions.

Unfortunately, I often see people taking Massive Action that is focused on only one area. They end up achieving Massive Results in one area, but they don't achieve true happiness because they don't have what they want in other areas.

Finding the right place can be a difficult balancing act, but it starts with a high-level strategy. Once you've figured that out, then you can take Massive Action toward implementing the strategy. If you haven't figured out the right strategy, then take Massive Action to do that first!

Make sure all the pieces fit together and work well before working toward your goals.

I liken this to a Ferrari. It can be the best-made car on the market, but if it's missing a steering wheel or a tire, it won't be much use to you. Just like in life, even if most of the parts are in perfect working order, missing even a few critical ones can lead to unhappiness.

Imagine you're building a house. You start with a *complete* set of plans drawn by an architect and engineer. Every little detail has been examined and planned so that your house comes together properly. Missing even one crucial item can lead to disaster.

To get the results you want in your life, make sure to carefully examine all the parts and pieces. Develop a high-level strategy that works together before you take Massive Action to implement the strategy.

# CHAPTER 31:
# LIVE WITH UNCERTAINTY

*"Life is the art of living with uncertainty, without being paralyzed with fear."*

—Dr. W. Dillon[27]

Taking Massive Action often creates uncertainty, because you're pushing yourself into new areas on many fronts. Tony Robbins (or Uncle Tony, as my kids call him) explains that successful people are very good at living with uncertainty, while people who have an average level of success need a high degree of certainty.

Decide what kind of person you are. If you crave certainty, you'll find it difficult to achieve a high level of success. You must get good—or at least comfortable—at living with uncertainty. This concept is similar to moving out of your comfort zone. People who are good at dealing with uncertainty move more easily out of their comfort zone.

My experience in medical school is a great example of this. I chose to attend medical school at a young age; I hadn't even thought about

---

27 Victoria Maxwell, "18 Quotes to Get You Through Instead of Going Under," *Psychology Today,* December 14, 2012, https://www.psychologytoday.com/blog/crazy-life/201212/18-quotes-get-you-through-instead-going-under.

all the options available. Becoming a doctor provided a great degree of certainty, which is one reason that many cultures and individuals (especially from my Indian background) value this career so highly.

My parents grew up in India during a time when certainty and security was at a premium, and they wanted financial security for themselves and their family. The economy was unstable, and there were few opportunities to get ahead. Becoming a doctor put you in a different class and was one of the only ways to get ahead in India during that time.

When you become a doctor, your future is quite certain. You graduate from medical school, you complete residency, then you start practicing. You'll have a job, and you'll make an above-average income. Once you decide your specialty, your income range is essentially set. It doesn't even really matter how good of a doctor you are, you will never worry about not having a job or income stream to support your family.

Compare this to careers in the arts or professional sports—in those fields, it's a completely opposite environment, with an extremely high degree of uncertainty. If you're the best in your field, you can earn millions; if you don't make the cut, you'll be waiting tables.

What level of uncertainty are you willing to live with? If you can tolerate a lot, you can achieve great things. If you're apprehensive about it, a more average life may work best for you.

You can improve your uncertainty tolerance by accepting that uncertainty is something you must learn to live with if you want to be successful. With practice, you can tell yourself every time you enter a highly uncertain zone that everything will be okay in the end. Either you will get the outcome you want or you will gain a great deal of experience that will make you stronger and better the next time around.

Once you understand this, you can free yourself up to take Massive Action and achieve great things in life. None of us really knows what our outcome will be in life, and learning to be okay with that uncertainty is important. Work hard at what you're doing, and live every moment for that moment.

Don't fool yourself into thinking that it's going to be an easy ride or a short journey. It's going to be a bumpy ride and take a long time. But if you want Massive Results, you must take Massive Action and be willing to endure the turbulence that will undoubtedly appear along the way.

"The quality of your life is directly related to how much uncertainty you can comfortably handle," Tony Robbins has said.

You must be able to live with uncertainty and the lack of security if you are to accomplish great things. You have to get used to uncertainty—even get comfortable with it. If you need safety and security, you're not the type of person who will become ultra-successful. You might be successful to a certain extent, but you will hit a ceiling. Remove your need for security, and you will remove the ceilings that prevent you from going higher. Be willing to swing big! Take Massive Action no matter what, and it will pay off.

# CHAPTER 32:
# MODELING

*Fortunately, most human behavior is learned observationally through modeling: from observing others.*
—Albert Bandura[28]

One of the common barriers to taking Massive Action is not knowing what to do. Once you decide to get serious, you may not know what to do, since your goal is likely something new and takes you outside of your comfort zone. Often, you don't even know where to start, and that can be paralyzing.

You genuinely want to take Massive Action, but you're just not sure what to do, where to go, or if you're even moving in the right direction.

One of the most powerful things to do in this situation is model: watch someone who has been successful in the way you want to be. The most important part of modeling is choosing to model someone who is truly at the top in the field you are interested in. Resist the urge to pick a more approachable, middle-of-the-road person.

---

28  Richard Culatta, "Social Learning Theory," InstructionalDesign.org, 2015, http://www.instructionaldesign.org/theories/social-learning.html.

It's human to relate better to more ordinary people, because we can more easily see ourselves doing what they have done. But this can be a big mistake. Model the absolute best, the number-one or number-two person in your chosen field. Also, look for a model that fits your personality and your goals as closely as possible. Model the best, and even if you only get halfway there, you will still have abundant success.

Many people struggle with this concept, even if they have adopted the modeling mind frame. They choose a successful model in their field, and everything seems good, except they have not chosen to model the front-runner. If you are going to invest the time and energy to take Massive Action, model the best. Don't overthink it, just follow your model exactly. Don't deviate, don't experiment—follow that model 100 percent.

A great example of this is online advertising. You might see an ad that works well, but maybe you think it's "old school" or even stupid. Your first instinct is that you could do this much better, so you set out to improve what's already working very well. Lo and behold, your new ad fails.

The original worked well, and perhaps the magic was that it looked old school and unsophisticated. Remember, when you first start modeling, do exactly what the other person is doing. Don't overthink it. They are successful for some reason, so initially your job is to figure out what they're doing—and follow that exactly. Once you become somewhat of an expert and gain your own experience and success, then you can start experimenting and changing up things. Until then, just model exactly.

I'm not talking about plagiarism or trying to imitate exactly. Follow the structure, the format, the essence of what they are doing, and when you start doing it, it will come out differently. When it is expressed through your unique being, it will be something wonderfully new yet retains the essence of what was successful.

Rajeev Ram is an Indian-American tennis player who has achieved a moderate level of success among the professional tennis ranks. He grew up idolizing Pete Sampras, arguably the best American tennis player of all time, and he copied Sampras's serve down to the exact detail. Ram's thinking was that if it worked so well for Sampras, it should work for him.

Of course, Ram's serve was never as good as Sampras's, likely because he copied it so completely. In the top ranks of professional tennis players, serves all look a bit different, although when you analyze them, they each have the same fundamentals. The trick is to keep the fundamentals but find the unique aspects of the serve that work best for your body and style of play.

Modeling will get you 90 percent of the way. It's easy to fall into the trap that you know better. If you knew better, you'd already be succeeding. You'd be the model for other people. There's a right time and place for trying new things, but at this new stage, stick to modeling those who have succeeded.

## CHAPTER 33:
# STAY IN PEAK STATE

*"Stay away from negative people. They have a problem for every solution."*

—Albert Einstein

Staying in peak state is another essential component that allows Massive Action to work its magic. When you're in the right state, it's relatively easy to achieve your goals. Things just flow.

So what's the right state? It's similar to what athletes call "the zone."

There isn't a specific formula or checklist to follow to reach peak state; it's more about consistently creating conditions that allow you to be in peak state. Those conditions vary from person to person, but generally staying focused, finding clarity, staying positive, removing negatives, and taking Massive Action create the conditions necessary for peak state.

You can't control everything all the time, thus guaranteeing that you can reach peak state whenever you want. But you can certainly create an environment that invites and welcomes peak state. Much like taking advantage of small wins to create momentum, when you continually optimize the conditions around you, you will find yourself in peak state more often.

The motivational speaker Charlotte Gambill coined the phrase "Own your zone."[29] It's a great mantra to remind yourself that *you* control your state of mind and the optimal zone for your peak performance.

Performance is maximized when athletes are "in the zone." Mark Calcavecchia, a major winning golfer, once said, "When I'm in a zone, I don't think about the shot or the wind or the distance or the gallery or anything; I just pull a club and swing."[30]

Interestingly when athletes talk about "being in the zone," they recognize it in retrospect. When they are in the zone, they often don't even know it. It's the same with peak state.

When you are in peak state, your subconscious and conscious minds—which typically fight each other to some degree—are in perfect harmony. Your rational (conscious) mind aligns perfectly with your emotions (subconscious), and together they combine into a powerful force that makes you unstoppable.

If you ever take an improv class, you will learn about turning off your thinking brain and simply reacting. This is what Eckhart Tolle talks about in *The Power of Now*.[31] When you can be in the moment and react fully and completely to what is in front of you, you will be at your best. This is what improv actors do: they turn off their thinking minds, get into the zone, and just react. They're not necessarily trying to be funny, yet improv shows often have some of the best comedy around. These actors practice the skill of "being in the moment." Those who are skilled improve performers have learned that when you try to be funny, you are using your thinking brain, which is actually counterproductive and makes you not funny. The best comedy happens when you simply react in the "now." This is also

---

[29] Charlotte Gambill, *Turnaround God: Discovering God's Transformational Power* (Nashville: Thomas Nelson, 2013).
[30] Quoted in *Golf Digest*, October 2016, https://www.golfdigest.com/gallery/golf-mental-quotes#1.
[31] Eckhart Tolle, *The Power of Now: A Guide to Spiritual Enlightenment* (San Francisco: New World Library, 2010).

how life works and why I think everyone should take improv classes. The drive home this very point.

Being in peak state is important because it allows you to take Massive Action. When you're in peak stake—living in the moment with everything feeling right—your natural desire is to intensify your efforts. When you are in a non-peak state, your subconscious mind fights your conscious mind, and you feel resistance to taking Massive Action. Your mind will be filled with thoughts like, "It's not worth it" or "What's the point? Nothing I do ever works." These subconscious emotions boil up in the form of negative thoughts and prevent you from gaining peak state.

When you're in peak state, these types of thoughts don't enter your mind. Or if they do, you easily deal with them, and your mind gets back on track without any derailment of your forward momentum. Everything is flowing well and moving forward; progress is being made. You're taking Massive Action and enjoying results along the way to your ultimate high-level success.

Being in peak state provides the right mind frame and energy necessary to take Massive Action. If you don't have these two things, evaluate your situation to identify what is preventing you from taking the action you desire.

Too often, the challenges and disappointments of life bring us down. Negative things naturally effect our state. Monitoring where we are and taking the steps to ensure that, no matter how negative things become, we maintain a peak state is an essential part of taking Massive Action.

Financial struggles, physical ailments, emotional and mental issues—all these and more can take a toll on your state of mind. These challenges can take away your desire to take Massive Action. You're defeated and exhausted, and all you want to do is quit.

That's why monitoring your state and envisioning your high-level goals are crucial. Remember to play the movie or slide show of you achieving your goals. Doing this helps you stay in the proper state and gives you the energy and momentum you need to move toward your high-level goals.

When we start something new, we're often excited, and it's easy to stay in the right state. As time goes on, however, the state naturally wears down. The reality of how difficult the actual task is starts to sink in. The initial low-hanging fruit are replaced by ones that need more effort and attention. This process can cause your state to deteriorate, which then causes you to stop taking Massive Action. It becomes a vicious cycle that ends up stopping your entire momentum. Monitoring your state throughout the day becomes essential.

Remember: obstacles and negative feedback will always appear. Accept them and keep taking Massive Action and moving toward your high-level goals.

Yes, it can be difficult. But the first step is simple: monitor your state. The second step is fairly easy too: self-correct in small ways that prevent you from going off the deep end and crashing. Your state may not always be optimal, but when you monitor and self-correct, you can at least prevent major issues that completely derail your path to Massive Action.

Your state can turn into an upward spiral or a downward spiral. Sometimes I wonder if people who find themselves in a state of depression (not related to clear-cut medical issues) work their way into that state. Something bad happens that depresses their state, which causes less action, which then causes more depression, which allows more bad things to happen, which continues to depress their state. This vicious cycle drives you down. If you self-correct along the way, you can prevent such a downward spiral.

Recognizing the right state allows you to use the cycle to your advantage. Every time something good happens, make sure you allow that momentum to elevate your state. And when something bad happens, tell yourself it will be okay, and don't let your state go down. If you can't increase your state, at least stay at the same level; don't go backwards. Over time, this will slowly increase your state to an optimal place.

A lot of success boils down to your baseline state of mind. When you're living in a high state, things come more naturally, it's easier to take Massive Action, and you just seem to have more success and results. The right state is one of the reasons certain people just accomplish a lot and are successful, while others don't. It's about staying in that right state and making the most of the natural flow that comes out of that.

Some people call this "high vibrational energy." When you have this kind of vitality, you're in the proper state, and you naturally attract positive things into your life. When you have "low vibrational energy," you repel good things and actually attract negative.

"Debbie Downer," a character on Saturday Night Live years ago, was the embodiment of low vibrational energy. Everything she did was a disaster, and nobody wanted to be around her. Low energy can be contagious—and so can high energy. Stay in that positive state that makes people want to be around you, and you'll find that you can stay on the path to Massive Action much more easily.

# CHAPTER 34:
# BELIEVE IN YOUR GOALS

*"Man is what he believes."*

—Anton Chekhov

Another important piece of taking Massive Action is to have the right belief and certainty in your goals. Without belief and certainty, Massive Action will not work. You must have a high degree of belief in what you're doing, that rock-solid inner-core belief (RSICB) that we discussed earlier. This allows your Massive Action to be the most effective possible. If your belief is anything less than a rock-solid inner-core belief, your efforts have a high chance of failing.

When you are on your journey, especially as you near the end and are close to success, your belief or lack thereof can sabotage you. You may not believe you can actually succeed or you may feel unworthy of the result. If so, you will find a way to sabotage yourself. Your subconscious might kick in and incapacitate you in ways you never imagined.

On the other hand, if you're taking Massive Action and you have RSICB, everything will flow more smoothly. If you truly don't believe, your journey will be more of a zigzag road because you'll be dealing with self-doubt along the way.

That's why establishing a rock-solid inner-core belief before you move forward becomes so important. It's the chicken-and-egg scenario: sometimes you must move forward and gain a level of success before you can get to that belief. That's when the fake-it-til-you-make-it approach works. Keep pushing yourself to have that solid belief—that will motivate you to take Massive Action and start getting results.

It's a weird mental dynamic, but when you truly believe something, it just starts happening. You can say the universe is helping you along, but I believe your actions simply get aligned and push in the same direction. Without this high-level belief, some of your actions are pushing forward and some backwards, and while you can still move toward success, it's like an uphill struggle. Once you truly believe, you start moving downhill, and it can be the difference between success and failure.

Clarity is also extremely important. You must have 100 percent certainty and clarity about what you want to do. If you're taking Massive Action, but you're unsure what you want to do with it, it's like taking two steps forward, then one step back. It's not an efficient way to do things. While you may achieve a moderate level of success, the big results require that you have 100 percent certainty and clarity on what you want and the action you are willing to take.

If you're not certain, your subconscious will doubt things, and you may not get the success you desire. Monitor your belief and your certainty, and make sure they are maximized. If you see deficiencies, work on those specifically. Take Massive Action to make sure that you have proper belief and certainty. This is a critical aspect of your success.

When positive things happen, run with that energy. Use it to create momentum so that you can have even more energy, and build upon that extra energy to take more Massive Action. Use that energy and momentum to create the high level of belief and certainty that you need.

Everything in life starts with a thought, even a simple thought like, *I'm hungry. What do I want for lunch? Hmmm, a Caesar chicken salad sounds great.* Then you take action toward getting that salad. It all starts with the thought that you're hungry.

Even before the thought, your state is important. What state you are in often determines the type of thoughts you have, and thoughts are the foundation for success: "As a man thinketh in his heart, so is he."[32]

Being in peak state equals peak performance. It allows you to properly take Massive Action toward your high-level goals. It establishes the foundation for your success.

Understanding and monitoring your state can be difficult. I find it helpful to obtain feedback. When I'm in social situations and receive positive feedback, I know I'm in the right state. Conversely, when I get a lukewarm reaction, I know my state is off. It has nothing to do with what I say or how I look or even how I'm acting—it is truly a function of my state of being. When I'm in the right state, I can say anything and people react positively. When I'm in the wrong state, I can say even great things and people don't react properly.

Some people struggle the most with this aspect of taking Massive Action. The important thing is to first recognize that being in the proper state is important. It's easy to get frustrated, and get down on yourself and feel overwhelmed by too many negative things. Focus on the positive, and work to correct the negatives as you stay in the peak state, knowing that as you're taking Massive Action, you'll reach your ultimate long-term goals and vision.

---

[32] Prov. 23:7 (KJV).

# CHAPTER 35:
# "PERSIST UNTIL"

*"I will persist until I succeed."*

—Og Mandino[33]

One thing that people who take Massive Action have in common is the "I will persist until" mentality. This mentality comes when you set your sights on a clear goal, typically a high-level goal, then simply persist until it is achieved, regardless of hard it is or how long it takes. This mindset is almost universal in those who succeed at a high level.

Conversely, I see the opposite mentality all the time—the "let's wait and see" mindset. If I get a certain score on the SAT, *then* I will apply to my dream school. If I can save enough money, *then* I will go on a cruise. If I have time, *then* I will exercise. This is absolutely the wrong attitude. If you want to attend your dream school, take the SAT as many times as you need. Do whatever it takes!

For example, if you want to become a doctor, you must be committed to do whatever it takes to graduate from medical school

---
33 Og Mandino, *The Greatest Salesman in the World* (New York: Bantam Books, 1968).

and complete your residency. Period. Nothing can get in your way. That's the "persist until" attitude.

People have said to me, "I'd love to be a doctor like you. If I get into medical school, then I'll become a doctor too." Sometimes they'll even have specific medical schools in mind. "If I get into this medical school, I'll become a doctor. It's close to home and convenient; I really like that. I don't want to move, so if I get accepted to a medical school more than four hours away, I'll just do something else."

Clearly these individuals do not have a burning passion to become doctors. Being a doctor sounds interesting—the opportunity to help people is always appealing, and the money is good. But being a doctor isn't tied into their big *why*.

Inevitably, you will fail on your journey to Massive Action, and certainly more than once. If Thomas Edison had the "let's wait and see" mentality, you'd be reading this book by candlelight.

When we analyze high achievers, they universally have this mindset—they set their minds on a goal, and they do not quit until the goal is reached. I call this the "pit bull" mentality. Pit bulls are genetically bred to attack at all costs. Once they go for something, attack is the only option; nothing else is acceptable. They refuse to stop until their target is neutralized. It's no coincidence that pit bulls have a reputation for being one of the most ferocious breeds of dogs. In fact, pit bulls are even banned from certain places and communities because they pose a danger.

Of course, I'm not suggesting you do anything dangerous—to you or anyone else. But understanding and adopting this mentality—"I'll do whatever it takes to accomplish my objective"—is essential to taking Massive Action and getting Massive Results.

Thankfully, anyone can train himself to have this mindset, and the process is simple and straightforward. It begins with one step. When you catch yourself thinking, "Oh, well, maybe this isn't working," just stop.

Remember it takes 10 years to master anything—I told you this wasn't easy. Evaluate where you are on this timeline, and make adjustments. If you've been working at your goal for three years and achieving good results but haven't reached the final prize, you're on the right track. Working at something for many years and not being where you want to be can be discouraging, but that's simply the way it works sometimes. Becoming a true master and achieving high-level goals takes time.

About four years after I started my homebuilding business, I experienced significant difficulties. The thought of quitting and doing something else crossed my mind regularly. In fact, that thought has been a significant problem throughout my life. Whenever I was working toward something and things got hard after a few years, I had a tendency to try something else. I am the perfect example of why understanding—and learning—this "persist until" mentality is so crucial. The real gold—the real reward—comes around the 10-year mark.

Understanding this as you begin the process is invaluable. You'll likely experience initial success early in your journey, but around that three- to five-year mark, you hit the "dip."

You'll feel tired and discouraged. You'll feel like you cannot go any further. This is exactly when you need to put your head down and persist. This is when you must push through no matter what. This is when your persistence will lead you to massive success. Author Seth Godin phrases it nicely when he says, "Never quit something with long-term potential just because you can't deal with the stress of the moment."[34]

It's easy to doubt yourself. It's easy to quit. You enjoyed initial results from taking Massive Action. But then the challenges get bigger, and it's discouraging. Recognize exactly where you are and that this is part of the process of taking Massive Action. If you're on track but hitting challenges, push through. Persist until you succeed.

---

34 Seth Godin, *The Dip: A Little Book that Teaches You When to Quit (and When to Stick)* (New York: The Penguin Group, 2007).

# SECTION III:
# HURDLES TO TAKING
# MASSIVE ACTION

## CHAPTER 36:
# THE INVISIBLE FORCE

*"We must do our work for its own sake, not for fortune or attention or applause."*

—Steven Pressfield

An invisible force often prevents us from doing the things we know are best for us. In his book *The War of Art*, Steven Pressfield describes this concept beautifully. He explains that our internal biological mechanisms want to keep homeostasis, or "the tendency toward a relatively stable equilibrium between interdependent elements."[35] The human body is all about keeping things within a certain range. Electrolytes in your bloodstream, for example, have to be kept within a certain very narrow range to sustain life. If they go too high or too low, you can die. Your body is a beautiful machine programmed for homeostasis, and every cell in your body will fight for it to sustain life. You have evolved over thousands of years to maintain balance, and in some ways, your life depends on it.

It's important to understand that if you want to accomplish great things in life and take Massive Action, your body's internal mechanisms

---
35  Steven Pressfield, *The War of Art* (Black Irish Entertainment, 2011).

will fight against you. I'm not talking about getting your electrolytes out of whack—I mean your body's internal *mental* programming will resist powerfully. When you start taking Massive Action, especially with something you really want, often an invisible force will appear that sabotages everything. You must be aware of, protect against, and ultimately fight against this force. It can be difficult at first, but over time, your body will realize that you're in control, and you are going to do this anyway, regardless of what it says.

The more you want something, the stronger the force can be. The more you want something, the more invested you are and the more the outcome means to you. This is when the force can be at its strongest—trying to protect you from a loss. You have built this goal up as so important in your mind that you have set yourself up for a big loss if you do not achieve it. Imagine instead something you don't really care about, something that doesn't matter whether you win or lose. Your subconscious mind picks up on this ambivalence, and the force that it creates behaves similarly. You don't care, so the force doesn't care either. It doesn't bother showing up, and thus you can achieve the task or goal easily. A common saying in sports—"You cannot want it too much"—accurately describes this phenomenon. You have to want something fiercely and work to break past this invisible force.

Compare the force to a child. Children will fight against something tooth and nail, but when their parents stand firm, over time children learn that it's not worth fighting for. Take going to bed, for example. Children finally resign themselves to just doing what their parents tell them to do and go to bed, because it's going to happen whether they fight or not. They might as well just make their peace with it.

Pressfield describes the force beautifully in his book. He writes, "Most of us live two lives: the life we live and the unlived life within us. Between the two stands the force." He notes the force can come in any shape or form. For me, it comes in the shape of an excuse. I have found myself all set to do something, and then somehow I find an excuse not to do it. In the moment, the pretext seems perfectly reasonable, but when I look back, I can see that I just didn't want to do it, or I was afraid of doing it.

The first step in overcoming this negative force is to recognize it. Understand that it's a real thing that exists and can prevent you from achieving at a higher level. It's something that arises from our genetics and subconscious but can be a powerful and real thing. You can't see it or touch it, but you sure can feel it when it arrives.

Imagine you're standing at the edge of a tall building. The closer you get to the edge, the more your body will resist and literally stop you from moving any closer. It's as if you are paralyzed, and your muscles will simply not move any further. The force will invoke fear and will overcome your rational mind. It will do whatever it takes to prevent you from getting too close to the edge. This is a purely genetic defense mechanism to keep you from dying—or protect you from doing something stupid.

Unfortunately, that defense mechanism can come into play just as strongly when we're trying to do something good. Take public speaking, for example. When confronted with that terror, many people describe the identical flight-or-fight response to an imminent death threat such as falling from a tall building or being chased by a tiger.

Fighting a diet can also invoke this powerful defense mechanism. You can show great discipline, but at the end of the day, your body is programmed to get the nourishment it thinks it needs. Over tens of thousands of years, your body has evolved to consume all the valuable nutrition it comes across when it's available. Take sugar for example: when you taste something sweet, it is often difficult to stop eating until it's all gone. Our ancestors evolved at a time when sugar was difficult to come by, and when they found it, their bodies told them to hoard it. Next time, try eating just one Reese's Cup in the pack of two. Let me know how it goes. Your body will fight you hard on this.

The only way to overcome this force is with time and determination. You must keep fighting with your body until it learns that *you* tell it what to do, not the other way around. You are in charge—not your body.

I know public speaking terrifies some people. They'll find every excuse not to do it, even though they know that being a good speaker is a useful skill. They'll even turn down free help, such as the Toastmasters program (a nonprofit organization that helps people improve their communication and public speaking skills in a supportive, nonthreatening environment). The program builds your self-confidence, polishes your speaking style, and teaches you how to engage with people. All these skills are extremely valuable in the business world. Very few people, however, take advantage of this essentially free resource because they're afraid of getting up and speaking in front of people. They will find every excuse under the sun: "It's not valuable," "I don't really need that," "I'll do it next year," etc. It's the invisible force.

Part of knowing yourself is understanding the kind of situations that summon this force. Once you recognize these events or situations, you can anticipate that the force will be extremely strong. You can start battling it from the beginning when you're not even in the situation or event. The awareness of this phenomenon allows you to take charge and eventually overcome it.

Do not expect instant results when you're battling the force. It takes time to overcome. Your body needs to learn that you're in charge, and it should consider the behavior you want as normal. Be aware of the force and learn to use it to your advantage instead of letting it control your life. Fight it and win, or it will prevent you from taking Massive Action and achieving massive success.

As they say in Star Wars, "May the Force be *with* you." Don't allow it to be *against* you.

## CHAPTER 37:
# YOU ARE ENOUGH

*"You are the only one who can limit your greatness. Remember, you are enough."*

—Unknown

When taking Massive Action, one thing that can block your momentum is feeling like you are unworthy of a goal or you're not enough. Recognize and accept right now that *you are enough!* You are worthy and capable of achieving whatever you set your mind to. You may not currently have the mindset or skills needed to achieve your full potential, but you can develop those. You have the innate talent to achieve, and you are worth the success you seek.

All of us have great potential when we are aligned with our big *why*. We can achieve amazing things. We need to stop doubting ourselves, accept that we are enough, and then work to acquire the mindset and skills necessary for success.

Achieving the success you desire won't be easy—you must take Massive Action over a long period of time. In her book *Grit: The Power of Passion and Perseverance*, Angela Duckworth notes, "as much as talent counts, effort counts twice."³⁶ Decide that you are enough, stop doubting yourself, and commit to the effort. As Henry Ford said, "Whether you think you can or think you can't—you're right."³⁷

It took more than 13 years for me to finally feel confident in my abilities as a top-notch emergency medicine physician. Four years of medical school, four years of residency, and about five years of actual practice before I knew I could take care of any type of patient who showed up on my doorstep.

Along the way, I doubted myself and wondered if I could ever do this. The mountain looks pretty tall when you are standing at the base and contemplating the climb. Once you start making progress and experiencing small victories, however, the mountain gets smaller and smaller. Don't focus on the challenges; just keep climbing. If you are taking Massive Action and working toward your ultimate goal, you will reach the summit.

Always remember: you can achieve whatever you can imagine. The human mind is an amazing thing that can either help you climb or stop you dead in your tracks. As a conscious being, your job is to choose which it will be. Make that decision, and remove the mental barriers as they arise.

The invisible force I'm talking about can paralyze you. That negative power can make you believe that taking Massive Action will not work and that results are just not possible. This is an illusion. The solution is simple: you must move past this point and just keep taking Massive Action.

In medical school, it was extremely hard for me to talk to patients. At the age of 17, I started a six-year combined BS/MD program, and I was talking to patients in clinical rotations by the time I was 19. The pressure of pretending to know everything people expect a doctor to know at such a young age was overwhelming. Of course, it would be difficult for anybody, but at that age, it was even more challenging.

Looking back now, I realize it was hard for me to have a discussion

---

36 Angela Duckworth, *Grit: The Power of Passion and Perseverance* (New York: Scribner, 2016).
37 Erika Andersen, "21 Quotes from Henry Ford on Business, Leadership, and Life," *Forbes*, May 31, 2013, https://www.forbes.com/sites/erikaandersen/2013/05/31/21-quotes-from-henry-ford-on-business-leadership-and-life/.

with a patient because I felt like a fraud. I worried that patients would think I was just a kid, get angry, and kick me out of the room. Sure, I wore the white coat, but I lacked the confidence and mental conviction needed for success.

Students in medical school are not called doctors and do not introduce themselves that way. Nevertheless, we are expected to know what we're doing. Of course, when we first start, we have no idea what we are doing. Over time, practicing medicine got easier and easier, and I realized that as long as I was doing my best, most patients appreciated what I did for them. I learned that as long as I cared about them, they were grateful to have me there.

Looking back, I laugh when I think about how hard it was to even talk to a patient. It seems so ridiculously easy now—it's become one of the most basic, instinctive things I do as a doctor. At the time, though, it created an invisible barrier that almost overwhelmed me when I had to go into a patient's room by myself. I made up all kinds of excuses to avoid this situation, and it frequently hindered my clinical performance and grades.

We've all had similar experiences when we first tried something that felt nearly impossible. After taking Massive Action and talking ourselves into doing it, we often look back and wonder why it was such a big deal.

Thinking about the problem often makes it seem even bigger and allows the insecurity of "Am I enough?" to creep in. This can become absolutely paralyzing and cause you to stop dead in your tracks. Taking Massive Action helps you overcome this fear—you stop thinking and start *doing* the things that will lead you to the success you want.

## CHAPTER 38:
# NEGATIVE FEEDBACK

*"Negative feedback can make us bitter or better."*
—Robin Sharma

When you start becoming a person who takes Massive Action at the right level, you will invariably start getting negative feedback—it just comes with the territory. Friends and family start wondering what the heck you're doing!

Usually, the people who love you just have your best interests at heart—they're genuinely confused and concerned that you're behaving so uncharacteristically. Some might even think you're being too risky.

When I left medicine, for example, my mom had a difficult time with my decision and was worried about me. The vast majority of people who go to medical school do so to become physicians, and they have lifelong careers in medicine. The truth is that many physicians are disgruntled with the medical profession for a variety of reasons, and wish they were doing something else. Very few leave medicine, though; the barriers to change are tremendous.

It took me about eight years to develop a different income stream that could replace my medical income. Along the way, many people—including my own mother—told me it was not the right path.

"Why would you spend all that time in medical school and residency just to give up?" she asked.

My decision to switch careers was so uncommon that they could not comprehend it and thus labeled it as negative—what most of us tend to do when we don't understand something. People are often afraid of something that's outside the norm. When you move outside your comfort zone, people will tell you not to do it, it's too risky, it'll never work. That's precisely when you need to continue.

Someone who would rather be working or attending a conference on weekends and evenings is not normal. Your family and friends might worry that something else is going on. Sometimes they're just jealous: you will be using your newfound knowledge and skills to rocket past the average person who just hangs out on the weekends. People start seeing you taking action and moving towards your goals—and then they see themselves standing still and not doing anything to move towards their goals. They feel inferior, and that turns into jealousy. They'll do everything they can to bring you back down to a "normal" level, and often they do so unconsciously.

The best analogy I have ever heard for this situation is a basket of crabs. If you put a bunch of crabs in a basket, as soon as one tries to climb to the top and escape, you'll see the other crabs pulling it down. This is exactly what it's like when you're trying to improve yourself and take your life to new heights. Those closest to you will consciously or unconsciously try to bring you down. If you succeed, it makes them look and, more importantly, feel inferior.

The best solution is to just to separate yourself from these people, even if they are longtime friends and family. This can be a difficult situation, because the negative feedback might get worse. You'll be hearing things like, "He thinks he's too good for us" or "What's gotten into her? I thought we were friends." Even your family may give negative feedback, since you're not going to be as close to them as you used to be. It's a difficult line to navigate, but it must be done. If you want to be another crab pulled down, then continue down this path. Otherwise make the difficult decision to distance or even separate yourself from those who are clearly bringing you down.

While it doesn't have to be a complete separation, you must put enough distance between you so that their negative thoughts and emotions don't affect you. It's been said that no matter how mentally strong you are, you are the sum of the five people you spend the most time with. The more time you spend around naysayers, the more time it will take you to get out of the basket. Even if you convince yourself that you're immune to the negativity, it will unquestionably have an affect on you. Humans are never completely immune to negative feedback—the best course of action is to avoid it entirely.

Conversely, the more time you spend with positive people who have gotten out of the basket and understand the importance of taking Massive Action, the quicker you will be able to move forward toward achieving all your dreams and goals.

Negative feedback is just part of the game. Once you start getting it, you'll know you're doing something right. When it starts happening, sit back and smile and be happy—instead of the "normal" reaction of being sad, questioning yourself, and considering reverting back to your old ways. It's a sign of progress along the road to success.

Imagine you're taking a 300-mile road trip to New York City. After a few hours, you see a sign that reads, "New York City—100 miles." You know you're two-thirds of the way there and have made progress towards the goal of getting to New York City. You should be happy when you see the sign! Negative feedback is a sign saying, "You're on the way, baby!" Keep it up, and you'll be there in no time.

A friend of mine is a great example of this attitude. He's a songwriter who moved to Nashville with the dream of becoming a hit songwriter. Of course, he joined thousands of other people who had moved to Nashville with the same dream. These odds didn't deter him, though. My friend took Massive Action and showed grit, maintaining his dream and effort over time. He was approximately seven years into his journey—with not much to show for his decision—when his parents had an "intervention." They told him he was wasting his life and that he needed to go earn a professional degree so he could support himself and his family. They had been patient enough as he had pursued his dream, and now it was time to "get serious."

He conceded they were probably right but decided to give it one more year before "getting serious" with his life. In that eighth year, he finally wrote his hit song and broke out. What if he had quit after seven years? He was only a year away from what Malcolm Gladwell calls the "tipping point."[38] Thankfully, he didn't listen to the voices around him and continued to take Massive Action. He reached the magic moment when all his hard work and experience finally came together and yielded massive results: a number-one hit song.

It's been said that most unsuccessful people are unsuccessful because they quit when they were 90 percent of the way to success. It was certainly true in the case of my friend, and you've probably experienced it in your own life. Don't give up when the critics say you should "get serious" and move on with your life! As long as you're taking Massive Action, you'll always have well-meaning critics trying to discourage you.

If you can't handle criticism, do something safe and secure—the critics will disappear. If you're going to medical school to become a doctor, you won't find too many who will discourage you. But is that really what you want to do? If so, great. But if not, take Massive Action to figure out what you really want to do. Don't let the critics stop you; use them and their energy as motivation to redouble your efforts.

---

38 Malcolm Gladwell, *The Tipping Point: How Little Things Can Make a Big Difference* (New York: Back Bay Books, 2000).

# CHAPTER 39:
# BAD ADVICE

*"Never ask advice of someone with whom you wouldn't want to trade places."*

—Darren Hardy

I often find that people will tell you the exact opposite of good advice for your situation. The reason for that irony is that they are not coming from a "Massive Action and abundance" mentality. Instead, they're coming from a defensive, self-protection mentality.

Most people have not taken the time to thoroughly study these concepts and understand what it takes to create high-level success. They mean well, but a lot of people who give unsolicited advice are those who have achieved only low to moderate success in their lives. Such people are giving you advice based solely on what they know, which may not be a lot.

It's like your friend who is always giving out medical advice. He's not a doctor, but he watches medical shows and "knows a lot." (Just because he stayed at a Holiday Inn Express last night does not make him smart, no matter what the commercials say.) He has not put in the hard work and time that it takes to become a doctor, and he doesn't have the years of experience to give the right advice in the right situation. Only a doctor can give the right advice in a medical situation.

This highlights the importance of making sure you take advice from people who have clearly shown a high level of success. Seek out those who have been taking their own advice and are actually practicing what they preach—don't ask somebody who did something successful 10 years ago but hasn't followed it up with more success. The world is changing so quickly these days; what worked just a few years ago might be outdated and irrelevant today.

I typically find two types of mistakes people make when they take advice from someone. First, they take advice from people who have not shown any amount of success in the field they are giving advice on.

For example, if you're seeking advice on how to live an insanely awesome life—and specifically the right decisions to make at critical junctures—first see how people have lived their lives and what level of success they have achieved. Remember, the Massive Action mindset is about achieving high-level success. I would highly recommend only taking advice from people who have achieved what you consider a high level of success. Of course, it is up to you to determine what a "high level of success" looks like.

Second, many people take advice from others who may have "been there, done that," but not for the last 10 years. They achieved a high level of success a long time ago but now are "resting on their laurels." They are giving advice and making money, but the advice is 10 years old and likely not the right advice for the current time. They haven't done much since that one high-level success, yet now are "teaching" others.

Be careful here—look for people who are doing what they are teaching—and crushing it. Remember the world we live in is rapidly changing. Even six months is a long time these days. Make sure you're taking advice from people who are actually doing it right now and at a high level.

I want to be clear that people who give wrong advice are typically not coming from a negative place. They are sharing advice because they truly believe what they are saying is in your best interest. They're telling you what they've done in your same situation, but the problem is that it has led to average or below-average results.

Few people understand high-level success and what it takes to get there. Few people understand what true Massive Action is and the amount of effort required to achieve a high level of success.

Those who understand this can advise you properly in your situation. Those who do not understand will often give you the wrong advice. They will tell you to turn left when you clearly need to turn right.

It's important to recognize when a person giving you advice isn't qualified to offer it. Several years ago, I got divorced, and my parents were continuously trying to give me advice on the right path forward. My parents are moderately successful people—they've done well but haven't accomplished anything especially notable. They were giving similar advice to a friend of mine who was also going through a divorce at the time. In a private conversation, my friend praised my parents' good advice. For me, though, their advice was the exact opposite of the best course of action for me.

Now, my friend and I are quite different: I believe in taking Massive Action every day, and that's just not her. My parents' advice fit her personality but not mine. They were not able to distinguish the principle of "the right advice for the right person." Advice isn't "one size fits all." As a Massive-Action taker, you must be able to make this distinction. Robert Kiyosaki famously said, "Careful who you get advice from. I get advice from people who are where I want to be."[39]

Understand there is nothing wrong with not taking Massive Action and being average; it's just that the lack of Massive Action will lead to average results. If that's what you want, then there is nothing further to do.

The way you think about decisions can determine your level of success. For example, if you want to be a race car driver, but you get into an accident and are badly injured, do you decide to get back on the horse (or in the car), or do you walk away? You need to decide what type of lifestyle you want to live. As you do, make sure you take

---

39 Robert T. Kiyosaki, Facebook page, February 27, 2013, https://www.facebook.com/RobertKiyosaki/posts/10151522563311788.

advice from people who are successful in that area, people with whom you would gladly trade places.

Similarly, when you're taking general life advice, make sure those folks have achieved high-level success similar to what you want to achieve. These are the people who will be able to advise you the best.

Remember, there is no right or wrong answer in life. This is where most people try to make things black and white and say it's one way or the other. This is a simplistic way of thinking and easy for people understand. The problem, however, is that life is much more complex, and you must take a deeper dive if you want to understand the real answer.

The most important thing is to be aware of this phenomenon. Recognizing it is a large part of the battle. When you're taking Massive Action, you will be one of the select few who will now be on target to achieve massive success. People along the way who are not on this path will tell you things that are literally 180 degrees opposite of what you should be doing. Remember our teenager working in the video store? He was able to understand and ignore the wrong advice. Just be on the lookout and recognize it, and avoid this pitfall when it does come up.

## CHAPTER 40:

# BAD SHIT

*"Sometimes it's a little, sometimes it's a lot, but it's always there. Don't let the bad shit stop you."*

—Sunil Saxena, M.D.

One of the barriers to taking Massive Action can be when things are going poorly in your life. It's important to remember that these are the moments when you need to take *more* Massive Action and push through.

When bad shit is happening, it's easy to get paralyzed and focus 100 percent on the negativity. It takes you out of a good mental state. Being in a positive frame of mind is crucial to taking Massive Action and performing at a high level. It is imperative for proper decision-making. When you are in the wrong state, poor decisions are more likely. The trick is to stay in a high-performance state despite the fact that bad shit is happening. This is when it is the most difficult but also most critical.

Remember that every single person has bad shit going on. It's not just you. Most people are good at putting on a front. Even for the highest achievers, if you can get them in a moment of true sincerity, you will see that there is plenty of bad in their lives that they are not letting show.

Years ago I was attending a retreat for CEOs of companies with sales ranging from $1 million to about $30 million. The attendees were all Type-A personalities with a lot of energy. You could tell people were jockeying for position and trying to show themselves in the best light.

The moderator had instructed everybody to write down things they were struggling with in their lives on a small sheet of paper and pass them to the front. He shuffled them up and just randomly read some of them, without identifying the individuals. I was shocked to learn how much bad stuff those people were going through. Things like, "My marriage is about to end," "I have a sex addiction, "I'm addicted to drugs and alcohol, I don't know what to do," and "My business is failing, and I don't think I can get it back."

Remember, people are always going to put on a good front, and it's difficult to see what's going on under the surface. The bad shit is always there. The trick is that, despite the bad things, these people are maintaining the proper state and moving forward on all fronts, pushing the positives even harder and working to fix the negatives.

Everyone has a mix of good and bad going on all the time. It's a rarity when everything is going 100 percent perfect, and nothing bad is happening at that time. It's simply a matter of staying in the right state and dealing with everything as it comes. Don't overly focus on the negative, but don't ignore the negative, either. Give it the right amount of time and energy so all the positive doesn't get lost while you are dealing with the negative.

Even the people we look up to in this world—celebrities, athletes, etc.— have bad stuff going on. Whether you love him or hate him, Tiger Woods is a great example of still performing at a high level on the golf course while enduring the death of his father, who was a critical figure in his life, and a public scandal and divorce from 2006 through 2010. Golf is a particularly hard sport to dominate, and Tiger did just that during those years, finishing number one in the world each of those years, despite a very messy personal situation.

We must be able to compartmentalize and still perform our primary function at a high level. This is the same for everybody, celebrity or not. In your case, however, the world is likely not watching you go through the bad shit. That's a much better situation!

This is similar to the invisible force. What bad shit does is push you out of your proper mental state and cause you to not take action. It's the opposite of Massive Action. Often you feel helpless and paralyzed. You're not sure what to do with these problems, so you do nothing. The state of paralysis and helplessness is exactly what can keep you down and make the problems worse.

When you're going through bad stuff, it can feel like the worst thing in the world to you. If you just look around, however, it's easy to recognize that the problems you are facing could be so much worse. Taking a step back helps reframe your thoughts and helps you to understand that, while it feels bad at the moment, it's just stuff you have to get through.

In 2007, I got fired from my first job. Looking back I probably *should* have been fired, since it was a bad fit for me. I was working as an ER physician, and my heart was not in it. I was performing at a good level but wasn't really putting forward my best effort. I was not a fit for the group I was part of. At the time, I was shocked, and I felt that all the hard work I had put in for the last six years of being part of the group had evaporated. I felt unworthy, and it was a big blow to my ego.

Looking back, however, I can see that it was the best thing that could have happened to me. First, it was the wake-up call I needed. I needed to focus and figure out what I really wanted to do with my life. Second, despite feeling like my world had stopped, I was able to realize (took me about 30 days) that as a board-certified EM physician, I was highly employable and did not have to worry too much about feeding my family. Third, it gave me a new perspective on life, and I was able to leave emergency medicine two years later and pursue my true passions.

The critical point is that, while bad shit was happening, it was not nearly as bad as it felt, and it turned out to be one of the most positive points in my life. It did not feel that way at the time, but it was.

The older you get, the more you realize that these issues come and go. It's not like there is an end goal where everything will be 100 percent positive. We're just dealing with a new set of good things and bad things, and the goal is to maximize the good and minimize the bad. The good and bad never really go away, but we learn to optimize things in our favor by staying in the right state.

So no matter your current situation, take Massive Action towards your goals now. Don't let anything, including bad stuff going on your life, be an excuse to "do it later." This is a common excuse: "Once I get past this, then I'll do what I really want to do." The right answer is that if it is important to you, then you must do it right now regardless of what's going on. Take Massive Action *now*; don't let your current situation be an excuse.

This reminds me of someone who was telling me how important a recommendation letter was that he needed me to write on his behalf. If he only had this letter, it would change his life. I said, "Sure, I'll do it for you this weekend. Just meet me in the morning at my home office, and I'll type it out with you and hand you an original signed copy." Of course, he did not follow up and did not meet me. Two days later, he asked me to just email the letter. Obviously the letter was not as important as he was making out to be.

The point is that if something is truly important, you'll get it done. If someone said they had $1 million for you and all you had to do was come pick it up, I guarantee nothing would stop you. If your favorite celebrity offered to visit with you personally, you would drop everything and make it happen. Keep in mind what is really important to you, and make sure you are taking Massive Action around that goal to make it a reality.

Often we get distracted by life and focus too much energy on things that truly don't matter. This causes us to not push hard enough on the things that do really matter and have the highest level of importance.

It's critical to make a list of the high-level goals you need to accomplish that will make a significant change in your life. These are the game changers. You must review these every day and make sure you're giving them 100 percent priority in your life. It's important to put them in order of importance. Because when number three conflicts with number one and you must make a decision, you should always be choosing what's in the best interest of number one. These types of decisions must be made on a daily basis. Once you've committed to number one being the true top priority in your life, then you must always give it the top priority. It's the first thing you think about when you get up and the first thing you act on every day. You act on it first until everything related to it is done. Then, and only then, do you work on other objectives.

If it's your number one objective, no matter what other bad stuff is going on, this is where you need to be spending the required time and effort. Compartmentalize and put the bad stuff away for a while and just work on this.

For example, if you're in financial debt, the only true solution is to make more money. It's hard to focus on this when the debt collector is calling and you could potentially lose your home. You must have the mental clarity and focus to start a business or figure out other revenue streams. This is what needs to be done. The high performers all behave this way—they understand that success is the only thing that's going to get them out of failure. Success just makes everything better.

An athlete who is struggling professionally and personally can only get out of this by winning again. Winning solves almost all the problems in sports. Success solves almost all the problems in life.

# CHAPTER 41:
# LITTLE ACTION EQUALS LITTLE RESULTS

*"You may never know what results come of your action, but if you do nothing, there will be no result."*

—Mahatma Gandhi[40]

Little action equals little results, which equals decreased belief in yourself, which equals less action. This is the definition of a downward spiral—like water going down the drain in your bathtub. This is exactly what we want to avoid at all costs. Once it gets started, it swirls faster and faster until all the water disappears. Once it gets started, it can be difficult to stop, and it takes so much more effort to stop it and reverse course.

As soon as you recognize the downward spiral, put the brakes on *hard*. The longer you wait or ignore the signs, the more difficult it will be to even get back to the point where you started.

The typical person who doesn't take Massive Action becomes disgruntled over time. They haven't seen results, which has reinforced

---

40 Ashoka, "12 Great Quotes from Gandhi on His Birthday," *Forbes*, October 2, 2012, https://www.forbes.com/sites/ashoka/2012/10/02/12-great-quotes-from-gandhi-on-his-birthday/#1f93f76033d8.

their belief that no matter what they do, life will always be the same. This person takes no ownership of their situation, and blames everything and everyone for their lack of results. It's a hard pattern to reverse. If you see yourself doing this, start by recognizing it and reversing these negative patterns of thinking.

Blaming lack of results on external factors could not be further from the truth. All anyone needs to do to see results is to start taking Massive Action and then be patient.

When you start taking Massive Action, you won't necessarily see the effects in days or even weeks. It could take three to six months before you start seeing significant results. And in most cases, what you are working on now typically shows its effects two or three years down the road. The important thing is to believe that you will see results at some point—and that those results will be commensurate with the amount of action you take. The more massive your actions, the more massive your results.

I believe in the three-year cycle. Certainly I have longer-term goals that will take more than three years to accomplish, but I have found that planning in a three-year timeframe works best. Basically, in three years you can turn something around, or start from scratch and see major gains. You won't likely achieve mastery in this timeframe, but you'll make significant progress. Cameron Herold talks about this in *Double Double*, his book that shows how to double a company's profits in three years—and then expands the concept to show how you can double anything you want to accomplish.[41]

It's essential to not fall into the low-action state, a vicious downward spiral that leads to depression and complete lack of action. Conversely, taking Massive Action is an upward spiral that eventually leads to massive success as you fulfill your long-term vision.

It's up to you. Do you want to take Massive Action or little action? Whatever you decide will determine your results. Remember, this is a long-term game played over years and even decades, not something that is over in a few weeks or months.

Achieving mastery takes at least 10 years, and you must be taking

---

41 Cameron Herold, *Double Double: How to Double Your Revenue and Profit in 3 Years or Less* (Austin, TX: Greenleaf Book Group, 2011).

## Massive Action Equals Massive Results

Massive Action all along the way. It can be difficult to sustain it—that's why grit is crucial: maintaining Massive Action over a long period of time, even during periods where you may not be seeing massive results for months or even years. Continue to take Massive Action and push as hard as you can. This is what it takes to achieve long-term success.

It is not the most talented in the field who experiences Massive Results—it is the

one who is the most willing to take Massive Action and sustains that action over a long period of time. It's that simple. The low-action takers will not be the ones holding the gold medal at the end of the games.

# CHAPTER 42:
# AVOID VICTIM MENTALITY

*"I am not what happened to me. I am what I choose to become."*

—Carl Jung[42]

One critical warning as you're taking Massive Action: never have a victim mentality. Acting like a victim—and worse, *believing* you're a victim—twists your frame of mind, creating a huge roadblock for your Massive Action.

No matter what happens to you, how bad or unfair a situation is, do not assume the role of the victim. Situations can and will be unfair—life is unfair. But as soon as you assume the victim role, your progress is blocked. When you become a victim, you're trying to remove the responsibility for the situation from your shoulders. As you take Massive Action, you become the leader of your life—you control what happens to you. It is important to operate from an ownership perspective and not from a victim mentality. Jocko Willinik

---

42  Cheryl Ekyl, "What is the Meaning of Meaning?," *Psychology Today*, October 30, 2011, https://www.psychologytoday.com/blog/beautiful-grief/201110/what-is-the-meaning-meaning.

and Leif Babin, two former Navy Seals, wrote *Extreme Ownership*, which talks in detail about this exact concept. These two believe that the single most important thing for leaders to successfully lead teams is to take ownership of every situation despite the circumstances or who was responsible. This is the exact opposite of the victim mentality and is critical to understand if you want to successfully be the leader of your life.

Imagine you're playing a round of golf and doing well. You're about to win the tournament on the $18^{th}$ hole . . . when suddenly another person picks up your ball and walks away. The rules official says it's your fault and you are disqualified because the ball was moved. This situation was completely out of your control, but you suffer the consequences.

Almost everybody who knows the situation would be complaining and assuming a victim mentality. Even though you were not wrong, it's important to understand that you cannot assume the victim mentality—it does not help the situation. Move on and do what's in your best interest.

Nelson Mandela was an inspiring example of this concept. If you're familiar with his story, it's easy to see how he might feel wronged by the things that happened to him. He was imprisoned for more than 20 years, simply because he didn't agree with the South African government, and they felt threatened by his power. He persevered and kept the right mind frame, refusing to take on the victim mentality. He eventually emerged from jail and became president of the very country that imprisoned him.

This is a perfect albeit extreme example of why it's so important not to assume the victim mentality. If you do, even on the smallest level, it sucks your energy and places the blame somewhere else. It removes your personal responsibility and puts you in a mental state where you do not control your destiny. It tells your brain that even though you're taking Massive Action, nothing positive will come out of it. You have no control.

This can't be further from the truth. As soon as you start assuming the victim role, you're telling your brain, specifically your subconscious, that Massive Action is useless because you're a victim. Remember, losers have things happen *to* them, but winners make things happen. Will you act, or be acted upon?

The victim mentality stops you dead in your tracks toward success. No matter what the situation, take extreme ownership. Even if things were clearly not in your control, take ownership—it is the *only* path to move forward.

You might find it interesting, as you go through the day, to see if you're assuming the victim mentality in any form. If you look closely, you may well be. Every time you start doing this, stop yourself and remember that nothing good comes out of this mentality, even if you were completely wronged.

## CONCLUSION:
# DETERMINE YOUR DESTINY

> *"Your beliefs become your thoughts,*
> *your thoughts become your words,*
> *your words become your actions,*
> *your actions become your habits,*
> *your habits become your values,*
> *your values become your destiny."*
>
> —Mahatma Gandhi[43]

Mahatma Gandhi, one of the greatest humans to grace this earth, explained the process of taking Massive Action clearly and succinctly. We've definitely examined the process in more depth. If you've reached the last chapter of this book, you've read—and hopefully learned—much about taking Massive Action to achieve Massive Results.

On one hand, taking Massive Action isn't easy. We've examined the numerous challenges and obstacles you'll face as you choose to

---

43  Ashoka, "12 Great Quotes from Gandhi on His Birthday," *Forbes*, October 2, 2012, https://www.forbes.com/sites/ashoka/2012/10/02/12-great-quotes-from-gandhi-on-his-birthday/#1f93f76033d8.

take Massive Action in your life. You'll become discouraged, you'll get tired, you'll fail, you'll be afraid, people will hate . . . the list of reasons to quit is long.

On the other hand, taking Massive Action is straightforward. We've outlined the time-tested, proven steps you need to take to achieve the Massive Results you desire. Identify your *why*, swing big, develop your rock-solid inner-core beliefs, develop mini habits, accept 30-day challenges . . . the list of things you can do to ensure success is long.

Few things in your life will be more rewarding or worthwhile than learning how to implement the process of taking Massive Action. As you choose this way of life, you'll discover that almost anything is possible. You'll identify the things that matter most, set S.M.A.R.T. goals, and work hard to achieve those goals. And then you'll repeat the process throughout your life.

It is my sincere hope that this book has shown you how taking Massive Action allows you to achieve a high level of success. What I want to reinforce is that results only occur if this process becomes a lifestyle—something you're actually *addicted* to.

When you start taking Massive Action, you will see results—maybe not instantaneously, but they will come. Seeing the fruit of your hard efforts will help you become addicted to this lifestyle and mindset. You will start to realize that this is something you should have been doing all along, and you will naturally want to continue to do it for the rest of your life.

It's important is to look for and acknowledge the small wins along the way. These wins will help reinforce this mentality and will serve you positively for the rest of your life as long as you stick with it. Remember, this is a long-term game. Life is not a quick sprint but rather a marathon—a long race you must run for the rest of your life.

A healthy "addiction" to something has to come from within. Taking Massive Action is a lot of work, but it's work you can learn to enjoy. Even if you're not that type of person now, give it a try and get started. Initially it may be difficult because you'll be venturing out of your comfort zone. However, once you start seeing results, this will become something that you want to continue for the rest your life.

While the word "addiction" typically has a negative connotation, in this context it's definitely positive. Become addicted to developing incredible habits! Become addicted to having the right frame of mind and to staying in a positive state that fosters maximum productivity.

As I look back at my life, from my days as a shy medical student to my current focus on establishing an entrepreneurial business that I can run from anywhere in the world, the attitude and mindset I've shared with you in these pages has changed my life. I've worked hard, refused to quit, and focused on what matters the most to me. And by doing so, I'm living a life I could never have imagined years ago.

Regardless of your *why*—whether it's personal relationships or physical health or professional success or anything else—the process outlined in this book will help you take charge of your life and determine your own destiny.

You've got this!

# DOWNLOAD THE FREE AUDIO BOOK!

Just to say thanks for downloading our book, we'd like to give you the Audiobook 100% FREE!

Go to
www.saxenaspeaks.com/freeaudiobook

*Sunil Saxena, MD*

# BOOK DR. SAXENA
## TO SPEAK

Visit

www.saxenaspeaks.com

*Sunil Saxena, MD*

www.ingramcontent.com/pod-product-compliance
Lightning Source LLC
LaVergne TN
LVHW051558070426
835507LV00021B/2638